THE NEW CLASS

OTHER TITLES BY **MILOVAN DJILAS**
AVAILABLE FROM **HARCOURT BRACE JOVANOVICH, PUBLISHERS**

Conversations with Stalin

Land without Justice

The Leper and Other Stories

Memoir of a Revolutionary

Montenegro

Njegoš: Poet-Prince-Bishop

Parts of a Lifetime

The Stone and the Violets

Tito: The Story from Inside

The Unperfect Society:
Beyond the New Class

Wartime

THE NEW CLASS

AN ANALYSIS OF THE COMMUNIST SYSTEM

by
Milovan Djilas

A Harvest/HBJ Book
Harcourt Brace Jovanovich, Publishers
San Diego New York London

Library of Congress Cataloging in Publication Data

Djilas, Milovan, 1911–
The new class.
(A Harvest/HBJ book)
Reprint. Originally published: New York : Praeger, 1957.
1. Communism—Yugoslavia. 2. Communism—Soviet Union.
3. Communism. I. Title
HX365.5.D49 1983 335.4 82-25859
ISBN 0-15-665489-X

Printed in the United States of America
First Harvest/HBJ edition 1983
B C D E

Preface

All this could be told in a different way: as the history of a contemporary revolution, as the expression of a set of opinions, or finally, as the confession of a revolutionary. A little of each of these may be found in this document. But, even if this is an inadequate synthesis of history, opinions and memoirs, it reflects my effort to give as complete and as brief a picture as possible of contemporary Communism. Some special or technical aspects may be lost, but the larger picture, I trust, will be that much simpler and more complete.

I have tried to detach myself from my personal problems by not submitting to them. My circumstances are, at best, uncertain and I am therefore compelled to express my personal observations and experiences hastily; a more detailed examination of my personal situation might some day supplement and perhaps even change some of my conclusions.

I cannot describe all the dimensions of the conflict in the painful course of our contemporary world. Nor do I pretend to know any world outside the Communist world, in which I had either the fortune or misfortune to live. When I speak of a world outside my own, I do so only to put my own world in perspective, to make its reality clearer.

Almost everything in this book has been expressed somewhere else, and in a different way. Perhaps a new flavor, color, and mood, and some new thoughts, may be found here. That is something—in fact, quite enough. Each man's experiences are unique, worthy of communication to his fellow men.

The reader should not seek in this book some kind of social or other philosophy, not even where I make generalized statements. My aim has been to present a picture of the Communist world but not to philosophize about it by means of generalizations—even though I have sometimes found generalization unavoidable.

The method of detached observation seemed to me the most suitable one for presenting my material. My premises could have been strengthened and my conclusions could have been proved by quotations, statistics, and recitals of events. In order to be as simple and concise as possible, I have instead expressed my observations through reasoning and logical deduction, keeping quotations and statistics to a minimum.

I think my method is appropriate for my personal story and for my method of working and thinking.

During my adult life I have traveled the entire road open to a Communist: from the lowest to the highest rung of the hierarchical ladder, from local and national to international forums, and from the formation of the true Communist Party and organization of the revolution to the establishment of the so-called socialist society. No one compelled me to embrace or to reject Communism. I made my own decision according to my convictions, freely, in so far as a man can be free. Even though I was disillusioned, I do not belong to those whose disillusionment was sharp and extreme. I cut myself off gradually and consciously, building up the picture and conclusions I present in this book. As I became increasingly estranged from the reality of contemporary Communism, I came closer to the idea of democratic socialism. This personal evolution is also reflected in this book, although the book's primary purpose is not to trace this evolution.

I consider it superfluous to criticize Communism as an idea. The ideas of equality and brotherhood among men, which have existed in varying forms since human society began—and which contemporary Communism accepts in word—are principles to which fighters for progress and freedom will always aspire. It would be wrong to criticize these basic ideas, as well as vain and foolish. The struggle to achieve them is part of human society.

Nor have I engaged in detailed criticism of Communist theory, although such criticism is needed and useful. I have concentrated on a description of contemporary Communism, touching upon theory only where necessary.

It is impossible to express all my observations and experiences in a work as brief as this one. I have stated only the most essential of them, using generalizations where they were unavoidable.

This account may appear strange to those who live in the non-Communist world; it would not seem unusual to those who live in the Communist one: I claim no exclusive credit or distinction for presenting the picture of that world, nor for the ideas concerning it. They are simply the picture and ideas of the world in which I live. I am a product of that world. I have contributed to it. Now I am one of its critics.

Only on the surface is this inconsistent. I have struggled in the past, and am struggling now, for a better world. That struggle may not produce the desired results. Nevertheless, the logic of my action is contained in the length and continuity of that struggle.

CONTENTS

Origins

1.

The roots of modern Communism reach back very far, although they were dormant before the development of modern industry in western Europe. Communism's basic ideas are the Primacy of Matter and the Reality of Change, ideas borrowed from thinkers of the period just before the inception of Communism. As Communism endures and gains strength, these basic ideas play a less and less important role. This is understandable: once in power, Communism tends to remodel the rest of the world according to its own ideas and tends less and less to change itself.

Dialectics and materialism—the changing of the world independently of human will—formed the basis of the old, classical, Marxist Communism. These basic ideas were not originated by Communist theorists, such as Marx or Engels. They borrowed them and wove them into a whole, thus forming, unintentionally, the basis for a new conception of the world.

The idea of the Primacy of Matter was borrowed from the French materialists of the eighteenth century. Earlier thinkers, including Democritus in ancient Greece, had expressed it in a different way. The idea of the reality of change, caused by the struggle of opposites, called Dialectics, was taken over from

Hegel; the same idea had been expressed in a different way by Heraclitus in ancient Greece.

Without going into the details of the differences between Marxist ideas and preceding similar theories, it is necessary to point out that Hegel, in presenting the idea of the Reality of Change, retained the concept of an unchanging supreme law, or the Idea of the Absolute. As he expressed it, in the last analysis there are unchangeable laws which, independently of human will, govern nature, society, and human beings.

Although stressing the idea of the Reality of Change, Marx, and especially Engels, stated that the laws of the objective or material world were unchangeable and independent of human beings. Marx was certain that he would discover the basic laws governing life and society, just as Darwin had discovered the laws governing living creatures. At any rate, Marx did clarify some social laws, particularly the way in which these laws operated in the period of early industrial capitalism.

This fact alone, even if accepted as accurate, cannot in itself justify the contention of modern Communists that Marx discovered all the laws of society. Still less can it justify their attempt to model society after those ideas in the same way that livestock is bred on the basis of the discoveries of Lamarck and Darwin. Human society cannot be compared to species of animals or to inanimate objects; it is composed of individuals and groups which are continuously and consciously active in it, growing and changing.

In the pretensions of contemporary Communism of being, if not the unique and absolute, but in any case the highest science, based on dialectical materialism, are hidden the seeds of its despotism. The origin of these pretensions can be found in the ideas of Marx, though Marx himself did not anticipate them.

Of course, contemporary Communism does not deny the existence of an objective or unchanging body of laws. However, when in power, it acts in an entirely different manner toward human society and the individual, and uses methods to establish its power different from those its theories would suggest.

Beginning with the premise that they alone know the laws which govern society, Communists arrive at the oversimplified and unscientific conclusion that this alleged knowledge gives them the power and the exclusive right to change society and to control its activities. This is the major error of their system.

Hegel claimed that the absolute monarchy in Prussia was the incarnation of his idea of the Absolute. The Communists, on the other hand, claim that they represent the incarnation of the objective aspirations of society. Here is more than just one difference between the Communists and Hegel; there is also a difference between the Communists and absolute monarchy. The monarchy did not think quite as highly of itself as the Communists do of themselves, nor was it as absolute as they are.

2.

Hegel himself was probably troubled by the possible conclusions to be drawn from his own discoveries. For instance, if everything was constantly being transformed, what would happen to his own ideas and to the society which he wanted to preserve? As a professor by royal appointment he could not have dared, in any case, to make public recommendations for the improvement of society on the basis of his philosophy.

This was not the case with Marx. As a young man he took an active part in the 1848 revolution. He went to extremes in drawing conclusions from Hegel's ideas. Was not the bloody class struggle raging all over Europe straining toward something new and higher? It appeared not only that Hegel was right—that is, Hegel as interpreted by Marx—but also that philosophical systems no longer had meaning and justification, since science was discovering objective laws so rapidly, including those applicable to society.

In science, Comte's positivism had already triumphed as a method of inquiry; the English school of political economy (Smith, Ricardo, and others) was at its height; epochal laws were being discovered from day to day in the natural sciences; modern industry was carving out its path on the basis of scientific technology; and the wounds of young capitalism revealed themselves in the suffering and the beginning struggle of the proletariat. Apparently this was the onset of the domination of science, even over society, and the elimination of the capitalistic concept of ownership as the final obstacle to human happiness and freedom.

The time was ripe for one great conclusion. Marx had both the daring and the depth to express it, but there were no social forces available on which he could rely.

Marx was a scientist and an ideologist. As a scientist, he made important discoveries, particularly in sociology. As an ideologist, he furnished the ideological basis for the greatest and most important political movements of modern history, which took place first in Europe and are now taking place in Asia.

But, just because he was a scientist, economist, and sociologist, Marx never thought of constructing an all-inclusive philosophical or ideological system. He once said: "One thing is certain; I am not a Marxist." His great scientific talent gave him the greatest advantage over all his socialist predecessors, such as Owen and Fourier. The fact that he did not insist on ideological all-inclusiveness or his own philosophical system gave him an even greater advantage over his disciples. Most of the latter were ideologists and only to a very limited degree—as the examples of Plekhanov, Labriola, Lenin, Kautsky, and Stalin will show—scientists. Their main desire was to construct a system out of Marx's ideas; this was especially true of those who knew little philosophy and had even less talent for it. As the time passed, Marx's successors revealed a tendency to present his teachings as a finite and all-inclusive concept of the world, and to regard themselves as responsible for the continuation of all of Marx's work, which they considered as being virtually complete. Science gradually yielded to propaganda, and as a result, propaganda tended more and more to represent itself as science.

Being a product of his time, Marx denied the need for any kind of philosophy. His closest friend, Engels, declared that philosophy had died with the development of science. Marx's thesis was not at all original. The so-called scientific philosophy, especially after Comte's positivism and Feuerbach's materialism, had become the general fashion.

It is easy to understand why Marx denied both the need for and the possibility of establishing any kind of philosophy. It is harder to understand why his successors tried to arrange his ideas into an all-inclusive system, into a new, exclusive philosophy. Even though they denied the need for any kind of philosophy, in practice they created a dogma of their own which they considered to be the "most scientific" or the "only scientific" system. In a period of general scientific enthusiasm and of great changes brought about in everyday life and industry by science, they could not help but be materialists and to consider themselves the "only" representatives of the "only" scientific view and method, particularly since they represented a social stratum which was in conflict with all the accepted ideas of the time.

Marx's ideas were influenced by the scientific atmosphere of his time, by his own leanings toward science, and by his revolutionary aspiration to give to the working-class movement a more or less scientific basis. His disciples were influenced by a different environment and by different motives when they converted his views into dogma.

If the political needs of the working-class movement in Europe had not demanded a new ideology complete in itself, the philosophy that calls itself Marxist, the dialectical materialism, would have been forgotten—dismissed as something not particularly profound or even original, though Marx's economic and social studies are of the highest scientific and literary rank.

The strength of Marxist philosophy did not lie in its scientific elements, but in its connection with a mass movement, and most of all in its emphasis on the objective of changing society. It stated again and again that the existing world would change simply because it had to change, that it bore the seeds of its own opposition and destruction; that the working class wanted this change and would be able to effect it. Inevitably, the influence of this philosophy increased and created in the European working-class movement the illusion that it was omnipotent, at least as a method. In countries where similar conditions did not exist, such as Great Britain and the United States, the influence and importance of this philosophy was insignificant, despite the strength of the working class and the working-class movement.

As a science, Marxist philosophy was not important, since it was based mainly on Hegelian and materialistic ideas. As the ideology of the new, oppressed classes and especially of political movements, it marked an epoch, first in Europe, and later in Russia and Asia, providing the basis for a new political movement and a new social system.

3.

Marx thought that the replacement of capitalist society would be brought about by a revolutionary struggle between its two basic classes, the bourgeoisie and the proletariat. The clash seemed all the more likely to him because in the capitalistic system of that time both poverty and wealth kept increasing unchecked, on the opposite poles of a society that was shaken by periodic economic crises.

In the last analysis, Marxist teaching was the product of the industrial revolution or of the struggle of the industrial proletariat for a better life. It was no accident that the frightful poverty and brutalization of the masses which accompanied industrial change had a powerful influence on Marx. His most important work, *Das Kapital,* contains a number of important and stirring pages on this topic. The recurring crises, which were characteristic of the capitalism of the nineteenth century, together with the poverty and the rapid increase of the population, logically led Marx to the belief that revolution was the only solution. Marx did not consider revolution to be inevitable in all countries, particularly not in those where democratic institutions were already a tradition of social life. He cited as examples of such countries, in one of his talks, the Netherlands, Great Britain and the United States. However, one can conclude from his ideas, taken as a whole, that the inevitability of revolution was one of his basic beliefs. He believed in revolution and preached it; he was a revolutionary.

Marx's revolutionary ideas, which were conditional and not universally applicable, were changed by Lenin into absolute and universal principles. In *The Infantile Disorder of "Left-Wing" Communism,* perhaps his most dogmatic work, Lenin developed these principles still more, differing with Marx's position that revolution was avoidable in certain countries. He said that Great Britain could no longer be regarded as a country in which revolution was avoidable, because during the First World War she had become a militaristic power, and therefore the British working class had no other choice but revolution. Lenin erred, not only in his failure to understand that "British militarism" was only a temporary, wartime phase of development, but because he failed to foresee the further development of democracy and economic progress in Great Britain or other Western countries. He also did not understand the nature of the English trade-union movement. He placed too much emphasis on his own, or Marxian, deterministic, scientific ideas and paid too little attention to the objective social role and potentialities of the working class in more highly developed countries. Although he disclaimed it, he did in fact proclaim his theories and the Russian revolutionary experience to be universally applicable.

According to Marx's hypothesis and his conclusions on the subject, the revolution would occur first of all in the highly developed capitalist countries. Marx believed that the results of the revolution—that is, the new socialist society—would lead to a new and higher level of freedom than that prevalent in the existing society, in so-called liberal capitalism. This is understandable. In the very act of rejecting various types of capitalism, Marx was at the same time a product of his epoch, the liberal capitalist epoch.

In developing the Marxist stand that capitalism must be replaced not only by a higher economic and social form—that is, socialism—but by a higher form of human freedom, the Social Democrats justifiably considered themselves to be Marx's successors. They had no less right to this claim than the Communists, who cited Marx as the source of their idea that the replacement of capitalism can take place only by revolutionary means. However, both groups of Marx's followers—the Social Democrats and the Communists—were only partly right in citing him as the basis for their ideas. In citing Marx's ideas they were defending their own practices, which had originated in a different, and already changed society. And, although both cited and depended on Marxist ideas, the Social Democratic and Communist movements developed in different directions.

In countries where political and economic progress was difficult, and where the working class played a weak role in society, the need arose slowly to make a system and a dogma out of Marxist teaching. Moreover, in countries where economic forces and social relations were not yet ripe for industrial change, as in Russia and later in China, the adoption and dogmatization of the revolutionary aspects of Marxist teachings was more rapid and complete. There was emphasis on *revolution* by the working-class movement. In such countries, Marxism grew stronger and stronger and, with the victory of the revolutionary party, it became the dominant ideology.

In countries such as Germany, where the degree of political and economic progress made revolution unnecessary, the democratic and reformist aspects of Marxist teaching, rather than the revolutionary ones, dominated. The anti-dogmatic ideological and political tendencies generated an emphasis on *reform* by the working-class movement.

In the first case, the ties with Marx were strengthened, at least in outward appearance. In the second case, they were weakened.

Social development and the development of ideas led to a severe schism in the European socialist movement. Roughly speaking, the changes in political and economic conditions coincided with changes in the ideas of the socialist theorists, because they interpreted reality in a relative manner, that is, in an incomplete and one-sided way, from their own partisan point of view.

Lenin in Russia and Bernstein in Germany are the two extremes through which the different changes, social and economic, and the different "realities" of the working-class movements found expression.

Almost nothing remained of original Marxism. In the West it had died out or was in the process of dying out; in the East, as a result of the establishment of Communist rule, only a residue of formalism and dogmatism remained of Marx's dialectics and materialism; this was used for the purpose of cementing power, justifying tyranny, and violating human conscience. Although it had in fact also been abandoned in the East, Marxism operated there as a rigid dogma with increasing power. It was more than an idea there; it was a new government, a new economy, a new social system.

Although Marx had furnished his disciples with the impetus for such development, he had very little desire for such development nor did he expect it. History betrayed this great master as it has others who have attempted to interpret its laws.

What has been the nature of the development since Marx?

In the 1870's, the formation of corporations and monopolies had begun in countries where the industrial revolution had already taken place, such as Germany, England, and the United States. This development was in full swing by the beginning of the twentieth century. Scientific analyses were made of it by Hobson, Hilferding, and others. Lenin, in *Imperialism, the Final Stage of Capitalism,* made a political analysis, based mainly on these authors, containing predictions which have proved mostly inaccurate.

Marx's theories about the increasing impoverishment of the working class were not borne out by developments in those countries from which his theories had been derived. However, as Hugh Seton-Watson states in *From Lenin to Malenkov,** they appeared to be reasonably accurate for the most part in the case of the agrarian East European countries. Thus, while in the West his stature was reduced to that of a historian and scholar, Marx became the prophet of a new era in eastern Europe. His teachings had an intoxicating effect, similar to a new religion.

The situation in western Europe that contributed to the theories of Engels and Marx is described by André Maurois in the Yugoslav edition of *The History of England:*

> When Engels visited Manchester in 1844, he found 350,000 workers crushed and crowded into damp, dirty, broken-down houses where they breathed an atmosphere resembling a mixture of water and coal. In the mines, he saw half-naked women, who were treated like the lowest of draft animals. Children spent the day in dark tunnels, where they were employed in opening and closing the primitive openings for ventilation, and in other difficult tasks. In the lace industry, exploitation reached such a point that four-year-old children worked for virtually no pay.

* New York, Frederick A. Praeger, 1953.

Engels lived to see an entirely different picture of Great Britain, but he saw a still more horrible and—what is more important—hopeless poverty in Russia, the Balkans, Asia and Africa.

Technological improvements brought about vast and concrete changes in the West, immense from every point of view. They led to the formation of monopolies, and to the partition of the world into spheres of interest for the developed countries and for the monopolies. They also led to the First World War and the October Revolution.

In the developed countries the rapid rise in production and the acquisition of colonial sources of materials and markets materially changed the position of the working class. The struggle for reform, for better material conditions, together with the adoption of parliamentary forms of government, became more real and valuable than revolutionary ideals. In such places revolution became nonsensical and unrealistic.

The countries which were not yet industrialized, particularly Russia, were in an entirely different situation. They found themselves in a dilemma; they had either to become industrialized, or to discontinue active participation on the stage of history, turning into captives of the developed countries and their monopolies, thus doomed to degeneracy. Local capital and the class and parties representing it were too weak to solve the problems of rapid industrialization. In these countries revolution became an inescapable necessity, a vital need for the nation, and only one class could bring it about—the proletariat, or the revolutionary party representing it.

The reason for this is that there is an immutable law—that each human society and all individuals participating in it strive to increase and perfect production. In doing this they come in conflict with other societies and individuals, so that they compete with each other in order to survive. This increase and expansion of production constantly faces natural and social barriers, such as individual, political, legal, and international customs and relationships. Since it must overcome obstacles, society, that is, those who at a given moment represent its productive forces, must eliminate, change, or destroy the obstacles which arise either inside or outside its boundaries. Classes, parties, political systems, political ideas, are an expression of this ceaseless pattern of movement and stagnation.

No society or nation allows production to lag to such an extent that its existence is threatened. To lag means to die. People never die willingly; they are ready to undergo any sacrifice to overcome the difficulties which stand in the way of their economic production and their existence.

The environment and the material and intellectual level determine the method, forces, and means that will be used to bring about the development and expansion of production, and the social results which follow. However, the necessity for the development and expansion of production—under any ideological banner or social force—does not depend on individuals; because they wish to survive, societies and nations find the leaders and ideas which, at a given moment, are best suited to that which they must and wish to attain.

Revolutionary Marxism was transplanted during the period of monopolistic capitalism from the industrially developed West to countries of the industrially undeveloped East, such as Russia and China. This is about the time when socialist movements were developing in the East and West. This stage of the socialist movement began with its unification and centralization in the Second International, and ended with a division into the Social Democratic (reform) wing and the Communist (revolutionary) wing, leading to the revolution in Russia and the formation of the Third International.

In countries where there was no other way of bringing about industrialization, there were special national reasons for the Communist revolution. Revolutionary movements existed in semi-feudal Russia over half a century before the appearance of the Marxists in the late nineteenth century. Moreover, there were urgent and specific concrete reasons—international, economic, political—for revolution. The basic reason—the vital need for industrial change—was common to all the countries such as Russia, China, and Yugoslavia, where revolution took place.

It was historically inevitable that most of the European socialist movements after Marx were not only materialistic and Marxist, but to a considerable degree ideologically exclusive. Against them were united all the forces of the old society: church, school, private ownership, government and, more important, the vast power machinery which the European countries had developed since early times in the face of the constant continental wars.

Anyone who wants to change the world fundamentally must first of all interpret it fundamentally and "without error." Every new movement must be ideologically exclusive, especially if revolution is the only way victory can be won. And if this movement is successful, its very success must strengthen its beliefs and ideas. Though successes through "adventurous" parliamentary methods and strikes strengthened the reformist trend in the German and other Social Democratic parties, the Russian workers, who could not improve their position by one kopeck without bloody liquidations, had no choice but to use weapons to escape despair and death by starvation.

The other countries of eastern Europe—Poland, Czechoslovakia, Hungary, Rumania, and Bulgaria—do not fall under this rule, at least not the first three countries. They did not experience a revolution, since the Communist system was imposed on them by the power of the Soviet Army. They did not even press for industrial change, at least not by the Communist method, for some of them had already attained it. In these countries, revolution was imposed from the outside and from above, by foreign bayonets and the machinery of force. The Communist movements were weak, except in the most developed of the countries, Czechoslovakia, where the Communist movement had closely resembled leftist and parliamentary socialist movements up to the time of direct Soviet intervention in the war and the *coup d'état* of February 1948. Since the Communists in these countries were weak, the substance and form of their Communism had to be identical with that of the U.S.S.R. The U.S.S.R. imposed its system on them, and the domestic Communists adopted it gladly. The weaker Communism was, the more it had to imitate even in form its "big brother"—totalitarian Russian Communism.

Countries such as France and Italy, which had relatively strong Communist movements, had a hard time keeping up with the industrially better-developed countries, and thus ran into social difficulties. Since they had already passed through democratic and industrial revolutions, their Communist movements differed greatly from those in Russia, Yugoslavia, and China. Therefore, in France and Italy revolution did not have a real chance. Since they were living and operating in an environment of political democracy, even the leaders of their Communist parties were not able to free themselves entirely of parliamentary illusions. As far as revolution was concerned, they tended to rely more on the international Communist movement and the aid of the U.S.S.R than on their own revolutionary power. Their followers, considering their leaders to be fighters against poverty and misery, naïvely believed that the party was fighting for a broader and truer democracy.

Modern Communism began as an idea with the inception of modern industry. It is dying out or being eliminated in those countries where industrial development has achieved its basic aims. It flourishes in those countries where this has not yet happened.

The historical role of Communism in the undeveloped countries has determined the course and the character of the revolution which it has had to bring about.

Character of the Revolution

1.

History shows that in countries where Communist revolutions have taken place other parties too have been dissatisfied with existing conditions. The best example is Russia, where the party which accomplished the Communist revolution was not the only revolutionary party.

However, only the Communist parties were both revolutionary in their opposition to the *status quo* and staunch and consistent in their support of the industrial transformation. In practice, this meant a radical destruction of established ownership relations. No other party went so far in this respect. None was "industrial" to that degree.

It is less clear why these parties had to be socialist in their program. Under the backward conditions existing in Czarist Russia, capitalist private ownership not only showed itself incapable of rapid industrial transformation, but actually obstructed it. The private property class had developed in a country in which extremely powerful feudal relationships still existed, while monopolies of more developed countries retained their grip on this enormous area abounding in raw materials and markets.

Czarist Russia, according to its history, had to be a latecomer with respect to the industrial revolution. It is the only European country which did not pass through the Reformation and the Renaissance. It did not have anything like the medieval European city-states. Backward, semi-feudal, with absolutist monarchy and a bureaucratic centralism, with a rapid increase of the proletariat in several centers, Russia found herself in the whirlpool of modern world capitalism, and in the snares of the financial interests of the gigantic banking centers.

Lenin states in his work *Imperialism, the Final Stage of Capitalism* that three-fourths of the capital of the large banks in Russia was in the hands of foreign capitalists. Trotsky in his history of the Russian revolution emphasizes that foreigners controlled forty per cent of the shares of industrial capital in Russia, and that this percentage was even greater in some leading industries. As for Yugoslavia, foreigners had a decisive influence in the most important branches of Yugoslav economy. These facts alone do not prove anything. But they show that foreign capitalists used their power to check progress in these countries, to develop them exclusively as their own sources of raw materials and cheap labor, with the result that these nations became unprogressive and even began to decline.

The party which had the historic task of carrying out the revolution in these countries had to be anti-capitalistic in its internal policy and anti-imperialistic in its foreign policy.

Internally, domestic capital was weak, and was largely an instrument or affiliate of foreign capital. It was not the capitalist class but another class, the proletariat which was arising from the increasing poverty of the peasantry, that was vitally interested in the industrial revolution. Just as the elimination of outrageous exploitation was a matter of life and death for those who already were proletarians, so was industrialization a matter of survival for those who in their turn were about to become proletarians. The movement which represented both of these had to be anti-capitalistic, that is, socialistic in its ideas, slogans and pledges.

The revolutionary party could not seriously contemplate execution of an industrial revolution unless it concentrated all domestic resources in its own hands, particularly those of native capitalists against whom the masses were also embittered because of severe exploitation and the use of inhumane methods. The revolutionary party had to take a similar stand against foreign capital.

Other parties were unable to follow a similar program. All of them either aspired to a return to the old system, to preservation of vested, static relationships; or at best, to gradual and peaceful development. Even the parties which were anti-capitalistic, as for example the SRs (Socialist-Revolutionary Party) in Russia, aspired toward returning society to idyllic primitive peasant life. Even the socialist parties such as the Mensheviks in Russia did not go farther than to push for the violent overthrow of the barriers to free capitalist development. They took the point of view that it was necessary to have fully developed capitalism in order to arrive at socialism later. However, the problem here was different; both a return to the old system and unhampered development of capitalism were impossible for these countries. Neither solution was capable, under the given international and internal conditions, of resolving the urgent problem of further development of these countries, i.e., their industrial revolutions.

Only the party which was in favor of the anti-capitalist revolution and rapid industrialization had prospects for success. Obviously that party had to be, in addition, socialist in its convictions. But since it was obliged to operate under prevailing conditions in general, and in the labor or socialist movements, such a party had to depend ideologically on the concept of the inevitability and usefulness of modern industry as well as on the tenet that revolution was unavoidable. This concept already existed, it was necessary only to modify it. The concept was Marxism—its revolutionary aspect. Association with revolutionary Marxism, or with the European socialist movement, was natural for the party then. Later, with the development of the revolution and with the organizational changes in the developed countries, it became just as essential for it to separate itself from the reformism of European socialism.

The inevitability of revolution and of rapid industrialization, which exacted enormous sacrifices and involved ruthless violence, required not only promises but faith in the possibility of the kingdom of heaven on earth. Advancing, as others also do, along the line of least resistance, the supporters of revolution and industrialization often departed from established Marxist and socialist doctrine. However, it was impossible for them to shed the doctrine entirely.

Capitalism and capitalist relationships were the proper and at the given moment the inevitable forms and techniques by which society expressed its needs and aspirations for improving and expanding production. In Great Britain, in the first half of the nineteenth century, capitalism improved and expanded production. And just as the industrialists in Britain had to destroy the peasantry in order to attain a higher degree of production, the industrialists, or the bourgeoisie, in Russia had to become a victim of the industrial revolution. The participants and the forms were different, but the law was the same in both cases.

In both instances socialism was inevitable—as a slogan and pledge, as a faith and a lofty ideal, and, in fact, as a particular form of government and ownership which would facilitate the industrial revolution and make possible improvement and expansion of production.

2.

All the revolutions of the past originated after new economic or social relationships had begun to prevail, and the old political system had become the sole obstacle to further development.

None of these revolutions sought anything other than the destruction of the old political forms and an opening of the way for already mature social forces and relationships existing in the old society. Even in those cases where the revolutionists desired something else, such as the building of economic and social relationships by means of force, as did the Jacobins in the French revolution, they had to accept failure and be swiftly eliminated.

In all previous revolutions, force and violence appeared predominantly as a consequence, as an instrument of new but already prevailing economic and social forces and relationships. Even when force and violence surpassed proper limits during the course of a revolution, in the final analysis the revolutionary forces had to be directed toward a positive and attainable goal. In these cases terror and despotism might have been inevitable but solely temporary manifestations.

All so-called *bourgeois* revolutions, whether achieved from below, i.e., with participation of the masses as in France, or from above, i.e., by *coup d'état* as in Germany under Bismarck, had to end up in political democracy. That is understandable. Their task was chiefly to destroy the old despotic political system, and to permit the establishment of political relationships which would be adequate for already existing economic and other needs, particularly those concerning the free production of goods.

The case is entirely different with contemporary Communist revolutions. These revolutions did not occur because new, let us say socialist, relationships were already existing in the economy, or because capitalism was "overdeveloped." On the contrary. They did occur because capitalism was not fully developed and because it was not able to carry out the industrial transformation of the country.

In France capitalism had already prevailed in the economy,

in social relationships, and even in the public conscience prior to inception of the revolution. The case is hardly comparable with socialism in Russia, China, or Yugoslavia.

The leaders of the Russian revolution themselves were aware of this fact. Speaking at the Seventh Congress of the Russian Communist Party on March 7, 1918, while the revolution was still in progress, Lenin said:

> . . . One of the fundamental differences between bourgeois and socialist revolutions is that in a bourgeois revolution, which arises from feudalism, new economic organizations which gradually change all aspects of feudal society are progressively created in the midst of the old order. In accomplishing this task, every bourgeois revolution accomplishes all that is required of it: it hastens the growth of capitalism.
>
> A socialist revolution is in an entirely different situation. To the extent that a country which had to begin a socialist revolution, because of the vagaries of history, is backward, the transition from old capitalist relations to socialist relations is increasingly difficult. . . .
>
> The difference between socialist revolutions and bourgeois revolutions lies specifically in the fact that, in the latter case, established forms of capitalist relations exist, while the soviet power—the proletariat—does not attain such relations, if we exclude the most developed forms of capitalism, which actually encompassed a small number of top industries and only very scantily touched agriculture.

I quote Lenin, but I could quote any leader of the Communist revolution and numerous other authors, as confirmation of the fact that settled relationships did not exist for the new society, but that someone, in this case the "soviet power," must therefore build them. If the new "socialist" relationships had been developed to the fullest in the country in which Communist revolution was able to emerge victorious, there would have been no need for so many assurances, dissertations, and efforts embracing the "building of socialism."

This leads to an apparent contradiction. If the conditions for a new society were not sufficiently prevalent, then who needed the revolution? Moreover, how was the revolution possible? How could it survive in view of the fact that the new social relationships were not yet in the formative process in the old society?

No revolution or party had ever before set itself to the task of building social relationships or a new society. But this was the primary objective of the Communist revolution.

Communist leaders, though no better acquainted than others with the laws which govern society, discovered that in the country in which their revolution was possible, industrialization was also possible, particularly when it involved a transformation of society in keeping with their ideological hypothesis. Experience —the success of revolution under "unfavorable" conditions—confirmed this for them; the "building of socialism" did likewise. This strengthened their illusion that they knew the laws of social development. In fact, they were in the position of making a blueprint for a new society, and then of starting to build it, making corrections here and leaving out something there, all the while adhering closely to their plans.

Industrialization, as an inevitable, legitimate necessity of society, and the Communist way of accomplishing it, joined forces in the countries of Communist revolutions.

However, neither of these, though they progressed together and on parallel tracks, could achieve success overnight. After the completion of the revolution, someone had to shoulder the responsibility for industrialization. In the West, this role was taken over by the economic forces of capitalism liberated from the despotic political chains, while in the countries of Communist revolutions no similar forces existed and, thus, their function had to be taken over by the revolutionary organs themselves, the new authority, that is, the revolutionary party.

In earlier revolutions, revolutionary force and violence became a hindrance to the economy as soon as the old order was overthrown. In Communist revolutions, force and violence are a condition for further development and even progress. In the words of earlier revolutionaries, force and violence were only a necessary evil and a means to an end. In the words of Communists, force and violence are elevated to the lofty position of a cult and an ultimate goal. In the past, the classes and forces which made up a new society already existed before the revolution erupted. The Communist revolutions are the first which have had to create a new society and new social forces.

Even as the revolutions in the West had inevitably to end in democracy after all the "aberrations" and "withdrawals," in the East, the revolutions had to end in despotism. The methods of terror and violence in the West became needless and ridiculous, and even a hindrance in accomplishing the revolution for the revolutionaries and revolutionary parties. In the East, the case was the opposite. Not only did despotism continue in the East because the transformation of industry required so much time, but, as we shall see later, it lasted long after industrialization had taken place.

3.

There are other basic differences between Communist revolutions and earlier ones. Earlier revolutions, though they had reached the point of readiness in an economy and a society, were unable to break out without advantageous conditions. We now know the general conditions necessary for the eruption and success of a revolution. However, every revolution has, in addition to these general conditions, its peculiarites which make its planning and execution possible.

War, or more precisely, national collapse of the state organization, was unnecessary for past revolutions, at least for the larger ones. Until now, however, this has been a basic condition for the victory of Communist revolutions. This is even valid for China; true, there the revolution began prior to the Japanese invasion, but it continued for an entire decade to spread and finally to emerge victorious with the end of the war. The Spanish revolution of 1936, which could have been an exception, did not have time to transform itself into a purely Communist revolution, and, therefore, never emerged victorious.

The reason war was necessary for the Communist revolution, or the downfall of the state machinery, must be sought in the immaturity of the economy and society. In a serious collapse of a system, and particularly in a war which has been unsuccessful for the existing ruling circles and state system, a small but well-organized and disciplined group is inevitably able to take authority in its hands.

Thus at the time of the October Revolution the Communist Party had about 80,000 members. The Yugoslav Communist Party began the 1941 revolution with about 10,000 members. To grasp power, the support and active participation of at least a part of the people is necessary, but in every case the party which leads the revolution and assumes power is a minority group relying exclusively on exceptionally favorable conditions. Furthermore, such a party cannot be a majority group until it becomes the permanently established authority.

The accomplishment of such a grandiose task—the destruction of a social order and the building of a new society when conditions for such an undertaking are not propitious in the economy or society—is a task able to attract only a minority, and at that, only those who believe fanatically in its possibilities.

Special conditions and a particular party are basic characteristics of Communist revolutions.

The achievement of every revolution, as well as of every victory in war, demands centralization of all forces. According to the Malthusian theory, the French revolution was the first in which "all the resources of a people at war were placed in the hands of the authorities: people, food, clothing." This must be the case to an even greater degree in a Communist "immature" revolution: not only all material means but all intellectual means must fall into the hands of the party, and the party itself must become politically, and as an organization, centralized to the fullest extent. Only Communist parties, politically united, firmly grouped around the center, and possessing identical ideological viewpoints, are able to carry out such a revolution.

Centralization of all forces and means as well as some kind of political unity of the revolutionary parties are essential conditions for every successful revolution. For the Communist revolution these conditions are even more important, since from the very beginning the Communists exclude every other independent political group or party from being an ally of their party. At the same time they demand uniformity of all viewpoints, including practical political views as well as theoretical, philosophical, and even moral views. The fact that the left-of-center SR's (Socialist-Revolutionaries) participated in the October Revolution, and that individuals and groups from other parties participated in the revolutions in China and Yugoslavia, does not disprove but rather confirms this proposition: these groups were only collaborators of the Communist Party, and only to a fixed degree in the struggle. After the revolution these collaborating parties were dispersed, or they dissolved of their own accord and merged with the Communist Party. The Bolsheviks routed the left-of-center SR's as soon as the latter wished to become independent, while the non-Communist groups in Yugoslavia and China that had supported the revolution had, in the meantime, renounced every one of their political activities.

The earlier revolutions were not carried out by a single political group. To be sure, in the course of a revolution individual groups pressured and destroyed one another; but, taken as a whole, the revolution was not the work of only one group. In the French revolution the Jacobins succeeded in maintaining their dictatorship for a brief period only. Napoleon's dictatorship, which emerged from the revolution, signified both the end of the Jacobin revolution and the beginning of the rule of the bourgeoisie. In every case, although one party played a decisive role in the earlier revolutions, the other parties did not surrender their independence. Although suppression and dispersion existed, they could be enforced only for a brief time. The parties could not be destroyed and would always emerge anew. Even the Paris Commune, which the Communists take as the forerunner of their revolution and their state, was a multi-party revolution.

A party may have played the chief, and even an exclusive, role in a particular phase of a revolution. But no previous party was ideologically, or as an organization, centralized to the degree that the Communist Party was. Neither the Puritans in the English revolution nor the Jacobins in the French revolution were bound by the same philosophical and ideological views, although the first belonged to a religious sect. From the organizational point of view the Jacobins were a federation of clubs; the Puritans were not even that. Only contemporary Communist revolutions pushed compulsory parties to the forefront, which were ideologically and organizationally monolithic.

In every case one thing is certain: in all earlier revolutions the necessity for revolutionary methods and parties disappeared with the end of civil war and of foreign intervention, and these methods and parties had to be done away with. After Communist revolutions, the Communists continue with both the methods and the forms of the revolution, and their party soon attains the fullest degree of centralism and ideological exclusiveness.

Lenin expressly emphasized this during the revolution itself in enumerating his conditions for acceptance in the Comintern:*

> In the present epoch of acute civil war, a Communist Party will be able to perform its duty only if it is organized in the

* *Selected Works,* Vol. X; New York, International Publishers, 1936.

> most centralized manner, only if iron discipline bordering on military discipline prevails in it, and if its party center is a powerful and authoritative organ, wielding wide powers and enjoying the universal confidence of the members of the party.

And to this, Stalin appended, in *Foundations of Leninism:**

> This is the position in regard to discipline in the party in the period of struggle preceding the achievement of the dictatorship.
>
> The same, but to an even greater degree, must be said about discipline in the party after the dictatorship has been achieved.

The revolutionary atmosphere and vigilance, insistence on ideological unity, political and ideological exclusiveness, political and other centralism do not cease after assuming control. On the contrary, they become even more intensified.

Ruthlessness in methods, exclusiveness in ideas, and monopoly in authority in the earlier revolutions lasted more or less as long as the revolutions themselves. Since revolution in the Communist revolution was only the first act of the despotic and totalitarian authority of a group, it is difficult to forecast the duration of that authority.

In earlier revolutions, including the Reign of Terror in France, superficial attention was paid to the elimination of real oppositionists. No attention was paid to the elimination of those who might become oppositionists. The eradication and persecution of some social or ideological groups in the religious wars of the Middle Ages was the only exception to this. From theory and practice, Communists know that they are in conflict with all other classes and ideologies, and behave accordingly. They are fighting against not only actual but also potential opposition. In the Baltic countries, thousands of people were liquidated overnight on the basis of documents indicating previously held ideological and political views. The massacre of several

* New York, International Publishers, 1939.

thousand Polish officers in the Katyń Forest was of similar character. In the case of Communism, long after the revolution is over, terrorist and oppressive methods continue to be used. Sometimes these are perfected and become more extensive than in the revolution, as in the case of the liquidation of the Kulaks. Ideological exclusiveness and intolerance are intensified after the revolution. Even when it is able to reduce physical oppression, the tendency of the ruling party is to strengthen the prescribed ideology—Marxism-Leninism.

Earlier revolutions, particularly the so-called bourgeois ones, attached considerable significance to the establishment of individual freedoms immediately following cessation of the revolutionary terror. Even the revolutionaries considered it important to assure the legal status of the citizenry. Independent administration of justice was an inevitable final result of all these revolutions. The Communist regime in the U.S.S.R. is still remote from independent administration of justice after forty years of tenure. The final results of earlier revolutions were often greater legal security and greater civil rights. This cannot be said of the Communist revolution.

There is another vast difference between the earlier revolutions and contemporary Communist ones. Earlier revolutions, especially the greater ones, were a product of the struggles of the working classes, but their ultimate results fell to another class under whose intellectual and often organizational leadership the revolutions were accomplished. The bourgeoisie, in whose name the revolution was carried out, to a considerable extent harvested the fruits of the struggles of the peasants and *sans-culottes*. The masses of a nation also participated in a Communist revolution; however, the fruits of revolution do not fall to them, but to the bureaucracy. For the bureaucracy is nothing else but the party which carried out the revolution. In Communist revolutions, the revolutionary movements which carried out the revolutions are not liquidated. Communist revolutions may "eat their own children," but not all of them.

In fact, on completion of a Communist revolution, ruthless and underhanded deals inevitably are made between various groups and factions which disagree about the path of the future.

Mutual accusations always revolve around dogmatic proof as to who is "objectively" or "subjectively" a greater counter-revolutionary or agent of internal and foreign "capitalism." Regardless of the manner in which these disagreements are resolved, the group that emerges victorious is the one that is the most consistent and determined supporter of industrialization along Communist principles, i.e., on the basis of total party monopoly, particularly of state organs in control of production. The Communist revolution does not devour those of its children who are needed for its future course—for industrialization. Revolutionaries who accepted the ideas and slogans of the revolution literally, naïvely believing in their materialization, are usually liquidated. The group which understood that revolution would secure authority, on a social-political-Communist basis, as an instrument of future industrial transformation, emerges victorious.

The Communist revolution is the first in which the revolutionaries and their allies, particularly the authority-wielding group, survived the revolution. Similar groups inevitably failed in earlier ones. The Communist revolution is the first to be carried out to the advantage of the revolutionaries. They, and the bureaucracy which forms around them, harvest its fruits. This creates in them, and in the broader echelons of the party, the illusion that theirs is the first revolution that remained true to the slogans on its banners.

4.

The illusions which the Communist revolution creates about its real aims are more permanent and extensive than those of earlier revolutions because the Communist revolution resolves relationships in a new way and brings about a new form of ownership. Earlier revolutions, too, inevitably resulted in major or minor changes in property relationships. But in those revolutions one form of private ownership superseded the others. In the Communist revolution this is not the case; the change is radical and deep-rooted, and a collective ownership suppresses private ownership.

The Communist revolution, while still in process of development, destroys capitalist, land-holding, private ownership, i.e., that ownership which makes use of foreign labor forces. This immediately creates the belief that the revolutionary promise of a new realm of equality and justice is being fulfilled. The party, or the state authority under its control, simultaneously undertakes extensive measures for industrialization. This also intensifies the belief that the time of freedom from want has finally arrived. Despotism and oppression are there, but they are accepted as temporary manifestations, to last only until the opposition of the expropriated authorities and counter-revolutionaries is stifled, and the industrial transformation is completed.

Several essential changes occur in the very process of industrialization. Industrialization in a backward country, especially if it has no assistance and is hindered from abroad, demands concentration of all material resources. Nationalization of industrial property and the land is the first concentration of property in the hands of the new regime. However, it does not, and can not, stop at this.

The newly originated ownership inevitably comes in conflict with other forms of ownership. The new ownership imposes itself by force on smaller owners who do not employ someone else's manpower, or to whom such manpower is unessential, i.e., on craftsmen, workers, small commercial merchants, and peasants. This expropriation of small property owners is effected even when it is not done for economic motives, i.e., in order to attain a higher degree of productivity.

In the course of industrialization, the property of those elements who were not opposed to, or even assisted, the revolution is taken over. As a matter of form, the state also becomes the owner of this property. The state administers and manages the property. Private ownership ceases, or decreases to a role of secondary importance, but its complete disappearance is subject to the whim of the new men in authority.

This is experienced by the Communists and by some members of the masses as a complete liquidation of classes and the realization of a classless society. In fact, the old pre-revolutionary classes do disappear with the completion of industrialization and collectivization. There remains the spontaneous and unorganized displeasure of the mass of the people—a displeasure which neither ceases nor abates. Communist delusions and self-deceit about the "remnants" and "influence" of the "class enemy" still persist. But the illusion that the long-dreamed classless society arises by these means is complete, at least for the Communists themselves.

Every revolution, and even every war, creates illusions and is conducted in the name of unrealizable ideals. During the struggle the ideals seem real enough for the combatants; by the end they often cease to exist. Not so in the case of a Communist revolution. Those who carry out the Communist revolution as well as those among the lower echelons persist in their illusions long after the armed struggle. Despite oppression, despotism, unconcealed confiscations, and privileges of the ruling echelons, some of the people—and especially the Communists—retain the illusions contained in their slogans.

Although the Communist revolution may start with the most idealistic concepts, calling for wonderful heroism and gigantic effort, it sows the greatest and the most permanent illusions.

Revolutions are inevitable in the lifetime of nations. They may result in despotism, but they also launch nations on paths previously blocked to them.

The Communist revolution cannot attain a single one of the

ideals named as its motivating force. However, Communist revolution has brought about a measure of industrial civilization to vast areas of Europe and Asia. In this way, material bases have actually been created for a future freer society. Thus while bringing about the most complete despotism, the Communist revolution has also created the basis for the abolition of despotism. As the nineteenth century introduced modern industry to the West, the twentieth century will introduce modern industry to the East. The shadow of Lenin extends over the vast expanse of Eurasia in one way or another. In despotic form in China, in democratic form in India and Burma, all of the remaining Asiatic and other nations are inevitably entering an industrial revolution. The Russian revolution initiated this process. The process remains the incalculable and historically significant fact of the revolution.

5.

It might appear that Communist revolutions are mostly historical deceptions and chance occurrences. In a sense this is true: no other revolutions have required so many exceptional conditions; no other revolutions promised so much and accomplished so little. Demagoguery and misrepresentation are inevitable among the Communist leaders since they are forced to promise the most ideal society and "abolition of every exploitation."

However, it cannot be said that the Communists deceived the people, that is, that they purposely and consciously did something different from what they had promised. The fact is simply this: they were unable to accomplish that in which they so fanatically believed. They cannot acknowledge this even when forced to execute a policy contrary to everything promised before and during the revolution. From their point of view, such acknowledgment would be an admission that the revolution was unnecessary. It would also be an admission that they had themselves become superfluous. Anything of the sort is impossible for them.

The ultimate results of a social struggle can never be of the kind envisaged by those who carry it out. Some such struggles depend on an infinite and complex series of circumstances beyond the controllable range of human intellect and action. This is most true of revolutions that demand superhuman efforts and that effect hasty and radical changes in society. They inevitably generate absolute confidence that the ultimate in human prosperity and liberty will appear after their victories. The French revolution was carried out in the name of common sense, in the belief that liberty, equality, and fraternity would eventually appear. The Russian revolution was carried out in the name of "a purely scientific view of the world," for the purpose of creating a classless society. Neither revolution could possibly have been created if the revolutionaries, along with a part of the people, had not believed in their own idealistic aims.

Communist illusions as to post-revolutionary possibilities were more preponderant among the Communists than among those who followed them. The Communists should have known and, in fact, did know about the inevitability of industrialization, but they could only guess about its social results and relationships.

Official Communist historians in the U.S.S.R. and Yugoslavia describe the revolution as if it were the fruit of the previously planned actions of its leaders. But only the course of the revolution and the armed struggle was consciously planned, while the forms which the revolution took stemmed from the immediate course of events and from the direct action taken. It is revealing that Lenin, undoubtedly one of the greatest revolutionaries in history, did not foresee when or in what form the revolution would erupt until it was almost upon him. In January 1917, one month before the February Revolution, and only ten months before the October Revolution which brought him to power, he addressed a meeting of Swiss Socialist youths:

"We, the older generation, perhaps will not live to see the decisive battles of the approaching revolution. But, I can, it seems to me, express with extreme confidence the hope that the youth, who work in the wonderful socialist movement of Switzerland and of the whole world, will have the good fortune not only to fight but also to emerge victorious in the approaching revolution of the proletariat."

How can it then be said that Lenin, or anyone else, was able to foresee the social results arising after the long and complex struggle of the revolution?

But even if Communist aims per se were unreal, the Communists, as distinct from earlier revolutionaries, were fully realistic in creating those things that were possible. They carried it out in the only way possible—by imposing their absolute totalitarian authority. Theirs was the first revolution in history in which the revolutionaries not only remain on the political scene after victory but, in the most practical sense, build social relationships completely contrary to those in which they believed and which they promised. The Communist revolution, in the course of its later industrial duration and transformation, converts the revolutionaries themselves into creators and masters of a new social state.

Marx's concrete forecasts proved inaccurate. To an even greater degree, the same can be said for Lenin's expectations that a free or classless society would be created with the aid of the dictatorship. But the need that made the revolution inevitable—industrial transformation on the basis of modern technology—is fulfilled.

6.

Abstract logic would indicate that the Communist revolution, when it achieves, under different conditions and by state compulsion, the same things achieved by industrial revolutions and capitalism in the West, is nothing but a form of state-capitalist revolution. The relationships which are created by its victory are state-capitalist. This appears to be even more true because the new regime also regulates all political, labor, and other relationships and, what is more important, distributes the national income and benefits and distributes material goods which actually have been transformed into state property.

Discussion on whether or not the relationships in the U.S.S.R. and in other Communist countries are state-capitalist, socialist, or perhaps something else, is dogmatic to a considerable degree. However, such discussion is of fundamental importance.

Even if it is presumed that state capitalism is nothing other than the "antechamber of socialism," as Lenin emphasized, or that it is the first phase of socialism, it is still not one iota easier for the people who live under Communist despotism to endure. If the character of property and social relationships brought about by the Communist revolution is strengthened and defined, the prospects for liberation of the people from such relationships become more realistic. If the people are not conscious of the nature of the social relationships in which they live, or if they do not see a way in which they can alter them, their struggle cannot have any prospect of success.

If the Communist revolution, despite its promises and illusions, is state-capitalist in its undertakings with state-capitalist relationships, the only lawful and positive actions its functionaries can take are the ones that improve their work and reduce the pressure and irresponsibility of state administration. The Communists do not admit in theory that they are working in a system of state capitalism, but their leaders behave this way. They continually boast about improving the work of the administration and about leading the struggle "against bureaucratism."

Moreover, actual relationships are not those of state capitalism; these relationships do not provide a method of improving the system of state administration basically.

In order to establish the nature of relationships which arise in the course of the Communist revolution and ultimately become established in the process of industrialization and collectivization, it is necessary to peer further into the role and manner of operation of the state under Communism. At present, it will be sufficient to point out that in Communism the state machinery is not the instrument which really determines social and property relationships; it is only the instrument by which these relationships are protected. In truth, everything is accomplished in the name of the state and through its regulations. The Communist Party, including the professional party bureaucracy, stands above the regulations and behind every single one of the state's acts.

It is the bureaucracy which formally uses, administers, and controls both nationalized and socialized property as well as the entire life of society. The role of the bureaucracy in society, i.e., monopolistic administration and control of national income and national goods, consigns it to a special privileged position. Social relations resemble state capitalism. The more so, because the carrying out of industrialization is effected not with the help of capitalists but with the help of the state machine. In fact, this privileged class performs that function, using the state machine as a cover and as an instrument.

Ownership is nothing other than the right of profit and control. If one defines class benefits by this right, the Communist states have seen, in the final analysis, the origin of a new form of ownership or of a new ruling and exploiting class.

In reality, the Communists were unable to act differently from any ruling class that preceded them. Believing that they were building a new and ideal society, they built it for themselves in the only way they could. Their revolution and their society do not appear either accidental or unnatural, but appear as a matter of course for a particular country and for prescribed periods of its development. Because of this, no matter how extensive and inhuman Communist tyranny has been, society, in the course of a certain period—as long as industrialization lasts—has to and is able to endure this tyranny. Furthermore, this tyranny no longer appears as something inevitable, but exclusively as an assurance of the depredations and privileges of a new class.

In contrast to earlier revolutions, the Communist revolution, conducted in the name of doing away with classes, has resulted in the most complete authority of any single new class. Everything else is sham and an illusion.

The New Class

1.

Everything happened differently in the U.S.S.R. and other Communist countries from what the leaders—even such prominent ones as Lenin, Stalin, Trotsky, and Bukharin—anticipated. They expected that the state would rapidly wither away, that democracy would be strengthened. The reverse happened. They expected a rapid improvement in the standard of living—there has been scarcely any change in this respect and, in the subjugated East European countries, the standard has even declined. In every instance, the standard of living has failed to rise in proportion to the rate of industrialization, which was much more rapid. It was believed that the differences between cities and villages, between intellectual and physical labor, would slowly disappear; instead these differences have increased. Communist anticipations in other areas—including their expectations for developments in the non-Communist world—have also failed to materialize.

The greatest illusion was that industrialization and collectivization in the U.S.S.R., and destruction of capitalist ownership, would result in a classless society. In 1936, when the new Constitution was promulgated, Stalin announced that the "exploiting class" had ceased to exist. The capitalist and other classes of ancient origin had in fact been destroyed, but a new class, previously unknown to history, had been formed.

It is understandable that this class, like those before it, should believe that the establishment of its power would result in happiness and freedom for all men. The only difference between this and other classes was that it treated the delay in the realization of its illusions more crudely. It thus affirmed that its power was more complete than the power of any other class before in history, and its class illusions and prejudices were proportionally greater.

This new class, the bureaucracy, or more accurately the political bureaucracy, has all the characteristics of earlier ones as well as some new characteristics of its own. Its origin had its special characteristics also, even though in essence it was similar to the beginnings of other classes.

Other classes, too, obtained their strength and power by the revolutionary path, destroying the political, social, and other orders they met in their way. However, almost without exception, these classes attained power *after* new economic patterns had taken shape in the old society. The case was the reverse with new classes in the Communist systems. It did not come to power to *complete* a new economic order but to *establish* its own and, in so doing, to establish its power over society.

In earlier epochs the coming to power of some class, some part of a class, or of some party, was the final event resulting from its formation and its development. The reverse was true in the U.S.S.R. There the new class was definitely formed after it attained power. Its consciousness had to develop before its economic and physical powers, because the class had not taken root in the life of the nation. This class viewed its role in relation to the world from an idealistic point of view. Its practical possibilities were not diminished by this. In spite of its illusions, it represented an objective tendency toward industrialization. Its practical bent emanated from this tendency. The promise of an ideal world increased the faith in the ranks of the new class and sowed illusions among the masses. At the same time it inspired gigantic physical undertakings.

Because this new class had not been formed as a part of the economic and social life before it came to power, it could only be created in an organization of a special type, distinguished by a special discipline based on identical philosophic and ideological views of its members. A unity of belief and iron discipline was necessary to overcome its weaknesses.

The roots of the new class were implanted in a special party, of the Bolshevik type. Lenin was right in his view that his party was an exception in the history of human society, although he did not suspect that it would be the beginning of a new class.

To be more precise, the initiators of the new class are not found in the party of the Bolshevik type as a whole but in that stratum of professional revolutionaries who made up its core even before it attained power. It was not by accident that Lenin asserted after the failure of the 1905 revolution that only professional revolutionaries—men whose sole profession was revolutionary work—could build a new party of the Bolshevik type. It was still less accidental that even Stalin, the future creator of a new class, was the most outstanding example of such a professional revolutionary. The new ruling class has been gradually developing from this very narrow stratum of revolutionaries. These revolutionaries composed its core for a long period. Trotsky noted that in pre-revolutionary professional revolutionaries was the origin of the future Stalinist bureaucrat. What he did not detect was the beginning of a new class of owners and exploiters.

This is not to say that the new party and the new class are identical. The party, however, is the core of that class, and its base. It is very difficult, perhaps impossible, to define the limits of the new class and to identify its members. The new class may be said to be made up of those who have special privileges and economic preference because of the administrative monopoly they hold.

Since administration is unavoidable in society, necessary administrative functions may be coexistent with parasitic functions in the same person. Not every member of the party is a member of the new class, any more than every artisan or member of the city party was a bourgeois.

In loose terms, as the new class becomes stronger and attains a more perceptible physiognomy, the role of the party diminishes. The core and the basis of the new class is created in the party and at its top, as well as in the state political organs. The once live, compact party, full of initiative, is disappearing to become transformed into the traditional oligarchy of the new class, irresistibly drawing into its ranks those who aspire to join the new class and repressing those who have any ideals.

The party makes the class, but the class grows as a result and uses the party as a basis. The class grows stronger, while the party grows weaker; this is the inescapable fate of every Communist party in power.

If it were not materially interested in production or if it did not have within itself the potentialities for the creation of a new class, no party could act in so morally and ideologically foolhardy a fashion, let alone stay in power for long. Stalin declared, after the end of the First Five-Year Plan: "If we had not created the apparatus, we would have failed!" He should have substituted "new class" for the word "apparatus," and everything would have been clearer.

It seems unusual that a political party could be the beginning of a new class. Parties are generally the product of classes and strata which have become intellectually and economically strong. However, if one grasps the actual conditions in prerevolutionary Russia and in other countries in which Communism prevailed over national forces, it will be clear that a party of this type is the product of specific opportunities and that there is nothing unusual or accidental in this being so. Although the roots of Bolshevism reach far back into Russian history, the party is partly the product of the unique pattern of international relationships in which Russia found itself at the end of the nineteenth and the begininng of the twentieth century. Russia was no longer able to live in the modern world as an absolute monarchy, and Russia's capitalism was too weak and too dependent on the interests of foreign powers to make it possible to have an industrial revolution. This revolution could only be implemented by a new class, or by a change in the social order. As yet, there was no such class.

In history, it is not important who implements a process, it is only important that the process be implemented. Such was the case in Russia and other countries in which Communist revolutions took place. The revolution created forces, leaders, organizations, and ideas which were necessary to it. The new class came into existence for objective reasons, and by the wish, wits, and action of its leaders.

2.

The social origin of the new class lies in the proletariat just as the aristocracy arose in a peasant society, and the bourgeoisie in a commercial and artisans' society. There are exceptions, depending on national conditions, but the proletariat in economically underdeveloped countries, being backward, constitutes the raw material from which the new class arises.

There are other reasons why the new class always acts as the champion of the working class. The new class is anti-capitalistic and, consequently, logically dependent upon the working strata. The new class is supported by the proletarian struggle and the traditional faith of the proletariat in a socialist, Communist society where there is no brutal exploitation. It is vitally important for the new class to assure a normal flow of production, hence it cannot ever lose its connection with the proletariat. Most important of all, the new class cannot achieve industrialization and consolidate its power without the help of the working class. On the other hand, the working class sees in expanded industry the salvation from its poverty and despair. Over a long period of time, the interests, ideas, faith, and hope of the new class, and of parts of the working class and of the poor peasants, coincide and unite. Such mergers have occurred in the past among other widely different classes. Did not the bourgeoisie represent the peasantry in the struggle against the feudal lords?

The movement of the new class toward power comes as a result of the efforts of the proletariat and the poor. These are the masses upon which the party or the new class must lean and with which its interests are most closely allied. This is true until the new class finally establishes its power and authority. Over and above this, the new class is interested in the proletariat and the poor only to the extent necessary for developing production and for maintaining in subjugation the most aggressive and rebellious social forces.

The monopoly which the new class establishes in the name of the working class over the whole of society is, primarily, a monopoly over the working class itself. This monopoly is first intellectual, over the so-called *avant-garde* proletariat, and then over the whole proletariat. This is the biggest deception the class must accomplish, but it shows that the power and interests of the new class lie primarily in industry. Without industry the new class cannot consolidate its position or authority.

Former sons of the working class are the most steadfast members of the new class. It has always been the fate of slaves to provide for their masters the most clever and gifted representatives. In this case a new exploiting and governing class is born from the exploited class.

3.

When Communist systems are being critically analyzed, it is considered that their fundamental distinction lies in the fact that a bureaucracy, organized in a special stratum, rules over the people. This is generally true. However, a more detailed analysis will show that only a special stratum of bureaucrats, those who are not administrative officials, make up the core of the governing bureaucracy, or, in my terminology, of the new class. This is actually a party or political bureaucracy. Other officials are only the apparatus under the conrol of the new class; the apparatus may be clumsy and slow but, no matter what, it must exist in every socialist society. It is sociologically possible to draw the borderline between the different types of officials, but in practice they are practically indistinguishable. This is true not only because the Communist system by its very nature is bureaucratic, but because Communists handle the various important administrative functions. In addition, the stratum of political bureaucrats cannot enjoy their privileges if they do not give crumbs from their tables to other bureaucratic categories.

It is important to note the fundamental differences between the political bureaucracies mentioned here and those which arise with every centralization in modern economy—especially centralizations that lead to collective forms of ownership such as monopolies, companies, and state ownership. The number of white-collar workers is constantly increasing in capitalistic monopolies, and also in nationalized industries in the West. In *Human Relations in Administration,** R. Dubin says that state functionaries in the economy are being transformed into a special stratum of society.

> . . . Functionaries have the sense of a common destiny for all those who work together. They share the same interests, especially since there is relatively little competition insofar as promotion is in terms of seniority. In-group aggression is thus minimized and this arrangement is therefore conceived

* New York, Prentice-Hall, 1951.

> to be positively functional for the bureaucracy. However, the esprit de corps and informal social organization which typically develops in such situations often leads the personnel to defend their entrenched interests rather than to assist their clientele and elected higher officials.

While such functionaries have much in common with Communist bureaucrats, especially as regards "esprit de corps," they are not identical. Although state and other bureaucrats in non-Communist systems form a special stratum, they do not exercise authority as the Communists do. Bureaucrats in a non-Communist state have political masters, usually elected, or owners over them, while Communists have neither masters nor owners over them. The bureaucrats in a non-Communist state are officials in modern capitalist economy, while the Communists are something different and new: a new class.

As in other owning classes, the proof that it is a special class lies in its ownership and its special relations to other classes. In the same way, the class to which a member belongs is indicated by the material and other privileges which ownership brings to him.

As defined by Roman law, property constitutes the use, enjoyment, and disposition of material goods. The Communist political bureaucracy uses, enjoys, and disposes of nationalized property.

If we assume that membership in this bureaucracy or new owning class is predicated on the use of privileges inherent in ownership—in this instance nationalized material goods—then membership in the new party class, or political bureaucracy, is reflected in a larger income in material goods and privileges than society should normally grant for such functions. In practice, the ownership privilege of the new class manifests itself as an exclusive right, as a party monopoly, for the political bureaucracy to distribute the national income, to set wages, direct economic development, and dispose of nationalized and other property. This is the way it appears to the ordinary man who considers the Communist functionary as being very rich and as a man who does not have to work.

The ownership of private property has, for many reasons, proved to be unfavorable for the establishment of the new class's authority. Besides, the destruction of private ownership was necessary for the economic transformation of nations. The new class obtains its power, privileges, ideology, and its customs from one specific form of ownership—collective ownership—which the class administers and distributes in the name of the nation and society.

The new class maintains that ownership derives from a designated social relationship. This is the relationship between the monopolists of administration, who constitute a narrow and closed stratum, and the mass of producers (farmers, workers, and intelligentsia) who have no rights. However, this relationship is not valid since the Communist bureaucracy enjoys a monopoly over the distribution of material goods.

Every fundamental change in the social relationship between those who monopolize administration and those who work is inevitably reflected in the ownership relationship. Social and political relations and ownership—the totalitarianism of the government and the monopoly of authority—are being more fully brought into accord in Communism than in any other single system.

To divest Communists of their ownership rights would be to abolish them as a class. To compel them to relinquish their other social powers, so that workers may participate in sharing the profits of their work—which capitalists have had to permit as a result of strikes and parliamentary action—would mean that Communists were being deprived of their monopoly over property, ideology, and government. This would be the beginning of democracy and freedom in Communism, the end of Communist monopolism and totalitarianism. Until this happens, there can be no indication that important, fundamental changes are taking place in Communist systems, at least not in the eyes of men who think seriously about social progress.

The ownership privileges of the new class and membership in that class are the privileges of *administration*. This privilege extends from state administration and the administration of economic enterprises to that of sports and humanitarian organizations. Political, party, or so-called "general leadership" is executed by the core. This position of leadership carries privileges with it. In his *Stalin au pouvoir*, published in Paris in 1951, Orlov states that the average pay of a worker in the U.S.S.R in 1935 was 1,800 rubles annually, while the pay and allowances of the secretary of a rayon committee amounted to 45,000 rubles annually. The situation has changed since then for both workers and party functionaries, but the essence remains the same. Other authors have arrived at the same conclusions. Discrepancies between the pay of workers and party functionaries are extreme; this could not be hidden from persons visiting the U.S.S.R. or other Communist countries in the past few years.

Other systems, too, have their professional politicians. One can think well or ill of them, but they must exist. Society cannot live without a state or a government, and therefore it cannot live without those who fight for it.

However, there are fundamental differences between professional politicians in other systems and in the Communist system. In extreme cases, politicians in other systems use the government to secure privileges for themselves and their cohorts, or to favor the economic interests of one social stratum or another. The situation is different with the Communist system where the power and the government are identical with the use, enjoyment, and disposition of almost all the nation's goods. He who grabs power grabs privileges and indirectly grabs property. Consequently, in Communism, power or politics as a profession is the ideal of those who have the desire or the prospect of living as parasites at the expense of others.

Membership in the Communist Party before the Revolution meant sacrifice. Being a professional revolutionary was one of the highest honors. Now that the party has consolidated its power, party membership means that one belongs to a privileged class. And at the core of the party are the all-powerful exploiters and masters.

For a long time the Communist revolution and the Communist system have been concealing their real nature. The emergence of the new class has been concealed under socialist phraseology and, more important, under the new collective forms of property ownership. The so-called socialist ownership is a disguise for the real ownership by the political bureaucracy. And in the beginning this bureaucracy was in a hurry to complete industrialization, and hid its class composition under that guise.

4.

The development of modern Communism, and the emergence of the new class, is evident in the character and roles of those who inspired it.

The leaders and their methods, from Marx to Khrushchev, have been varied and changing. It never occurred to Marx to prevent others from voicing their ideas. Lenin tolerated free discussion in his party and did not think that party forums, let alone the party head, should regulate the expression of "proper" or "improper" ideas. Stalin abolished every type of intra-party discussion, and made the expression of ideology solely the right of the central forum—or of himself. Other Communist movements were different. For instance, Marx's International Workers' Union (the so-called First International) was not Marxist in ideology, but a union of varied groups which adopted only the resolutions on which its members agreed. Lenin's party was an *avant-garde* group combining an internal revolutionary morality and ideological monolithic structure with democracy of a kind. Under Stalin the party became a mass of ideologically disinterested men, who got their ideas from above, but were wholehearted and unanimous in the defense of a system that assured them unquestionable privileges. Marx actually never created a party; Lenin destroyed all parties except his own, including the Socialist Party. Stalin relegated even the Bolshevik Party to second rank, transforming its core into the core of the new class, and transforming the party into a privileged impersonal and colorless group.

Marx created a system of the roles of classes, and of class war in society, even though he did not discover them, and he saw that mankind is mostly made up of members of discernible classes, although he was only restating Terence's Stoic philosophy: *"Humani nihil a me alienum puto."* Lenin viewed men as sharing ideas rather than as being members of discernible classes. Stalin saw in men only obedient subjects or enemies. Marx died a poor emigrant in London, but was valued by learned men and valued in the movement; Lenin died as the leader of one of the greatest revolutions, but died as a dictator about whom a cult had already begun to form; when Stalin died, he had already transformed himself into a god.

These changes in personalities are only the reflection of changes which had already taken place and were the very soul of the Communist movement.

Although he did not realize it, Lenin started the organization of the new class. He established the party along Bolshevik lines and developed the theories of its unique and leading role in the building of a new society. This is but one aspect of his many-sided and gigantic work; it is the aspect which came about from his actions rather than his wishes. It is also the aspect which led the new class to revere him.

The real and direct originator of the new class, however, was Stalin. He was a man of quick reflexes and a tendency to coarse humor, not very educated nor a good speaker. But he was a relentless dogmatician and a great administrator, a Georgian who knew better than anyone else whither the new powers of Greater Russia were taking her. He created the new class by the use of the most barbaric means, not even sparing the class itself. It was inevitable that the new class which placed him at the top would later submit to his unbridled and brutal nature. He was the true leader of that class as long as the class was building itself up, and attaining power.

The new class was born in the revolutionary struggle in the Communist Party, but was developed in the industrial revolution. Without the revolution, without industry, the class's position would not have been secure and its power would have been limited.

While the country was being industrialized, Stalin began to introduce considerable variations in wages, at the same time allowing the development toward various privileges to proceed. He thought that industrialization would come to nothing if the new class were not made materially interested in the process, by acquisition of some property for itself. Without industrialization the new class would find it difficult to hold its position, for it would have neither historical justification nor the material resources for its continued existence.

The increase in the membership of the party, or of the bureaucracy, was closely connected with this. In 1927, on the eve of industrialization, the Soviet Communist Party had 887,233 members. In 1934, at the end of the First Five-Year Plan, the membership had increased to 1,874,488. This was a phenomenon obviously connected with industrialization: the prospects for the new class and privileges for its members were improving. What is more, the privileges and the class were expanding more rapidly than industrialization itself. It is difficult to cite any statistics on this point, but the conclusion is self-evident for anyone who bears in mind that the standard of living has not kept pace with industrial production, while the new class actually seized the lion's share of the economic and other progress earned by the sacrifices and efforts of the masses.

The establishment of the new class did not proceed smoothly. It encountered bitter opposition from existing classes and from those revolutionaries who could not reconcile reality with the ideals of their struggle. In the U.S.S.R. the opposition of revolutionaries was most evident in the Trotsky-Stalin conflict. The conflict between Trotsky and Stalin, or between oppositionists in the party and Stalin, as well as the conflict between the regime and the peasantry, became more intense as industrialization advanced and the power and authority of the new class increased.

Trotsky, an excellent speaker, brilliant stylist, and skilled polemicist, a man cultured and of excellent intelligence, was deficient in only one quality: a sense of reality. He wanted to be a revolutionary in a period when life imposed the commonplace. He wished to revive a revolutionary party which was being transformed into something completely different, into a new class unconcerned with great ideals and interested only in the everyday pleasures of life. He expected action from a mass already tired by war, hunger, and death, at a time when the new class already strongly held the reins and had begun to experience the sweetness of privilege. Trotsky's fireworks lit up the distant heavens; but he could not rekindle fires in weary men. He sharply noted the sorry aspect of the new phenomena but he did not grasp their meaning. In addition, he had never been a Bolshevik. This was his vice and his virtue. Attacking the party bureaucracy in the name of the revolution, he attacked the cult of the party and, although he was not conscious of it, the new class.

Stalin looked neither far ahead nor far behind. He had seated himself at the head of the new power which was being born—the new class, the political bureaucracy, and bureaucratism—and became its leader and organizer. He did not preach

—he made decisions. He too promised a shining future, but one which bureaucracy could visualize as being real because its life was improving from day to day and its position was being strengthened. He spoke without ardor and color, but the new class was better able to understand this kind of realistic language. Trotsky wished to extend the revolution to Europe; Stalin was not opposed to the idea but this hazardous undertaking did not prevent him from worrying about Mother Russia or, specifically, about ways of strengthening the new system and increasing the power and reputation of the Russian state. Trotsky was a man of the revolution of the past; Stalin was a man of today and, thus, of the future.

In Stalin's victory Trotsky saw the Thermidoric reaction against the revolution, actually the bureaucratic corruption of the Soviet government and the revolutionary cause. Consequently, he understood and was deeply hurt by the amorality of Stalin's methods. Trotsky was the first, although he was not aware of it, who in the attempt to save the Communist movement discovered the essence of contemporary Communism. But he was not capable of seeing it through to the end. He supposed that this was only a momentary cropping up of bureaucracy, corrupting the party and the revolution, and concluded that the solution was in a change at the top, in a "palace revolution." When a palace revolution actually took place after Stalin's death, it could be seen that the essence had not changed; something deeper and more lasting was involved. The Soviet Thermidor of Stalin had not only led to the installation of a government more despotic than the previous one, but also to the installation of a class. This was the continuation of that other violent foreign revolution which had inevitably borne and strengthened the new class.

Stalin could, with equal if not greater right, refer to Lenin and all the revolution, just as Trotsky did. For Stalin was the lawful although wicked offspring of Lenin and the revolution.

History has no previous record of a personality like Lenin

who, by his versatility and persistence, developed one of the greatest revolutions known to men. It also has no record of a personality like Stalin, who took on the enormous task of strengthening, in terms of power and property, a new class born out of one of the greatest revolutions in one of the largest of the world's countries.

Behind Lenin, who was all passion and thought, stands the dull, gray figure of Joseph Stalin, the symbol of the difficult, cruel, and unscrupulous ascent of the new class to its final power.

After Lenin and Stalin came what had to come; namely, mediocrity in the form of collective leadership. And also there came the apparently sincere, kind-hearted, non-intellectual "man of the people"—Nikita Khrushchev. The new class no longer needs the revolutionaries or dogmatists it once required; it is satisfied with simple personalities, such as Khrushchev, Malenkov, Bulganin, and Shepilov, whose every word reflects the average man. The new class itself is tired of dogmatic purges and training sessions. It would like to live quietly. It must protect itself even from its own authorized leader now that it has been adequately strengthened. Stalin remained the same as he was when the class was weak, when cruel measures were necessary against even those in its own ranks who threatened to deviate. Today this is all unnecessary. Without relinquishing anything it created under Stalin's leadership, the new class appears to be renouncing his authority for the past few years. But it is not really renouncing that authority—only Stalin's methods which, according to Khrushchev, hurt "good Communists."

Lenin's revolutionary epoch was replaced by Stalin's epoch, in which authority and ownership, and industrialization, were strengthened so that the much desired peaceful and good life of the new class could begin. Lenin's *revolutionary* Communism was replaced by Stalin's *dogmatic* communism, which in turn was replaced by *non-dogmatic* Communism, a so-called collective leadership or a group of oligarchs.

These are the three phases of development of the new class in the U.S.S.R. or of Russian Communism (or of every other type of Communism in one manner or another).

The fate of Yugoslav Communism was to unify these three phases in the single personality of Tito, along with national and personal characteristics. Tito is a great revolutionary, but without original ideas; he has attained personal power, but without Stalin's distrustfulness and dogmatism. Like Khrushchev, Tito is a representative of the people, that is, of the middle-party strata. The road which Yugoslav Communism has traveled—attaining a revolution, copying Stalinism, then renouncing Stalinism and seeking its own form—is seen most fully in the personality of Tito. Yugoslav Communism has been more consistent than other parties in preserving the substance of Communism, yet never renouncing any form which could be of value to it.

The three phases in the development of the new class—Lenin, Stalin, and "collective leadership"—are not completely divorced from each other, in substance or in ideas.

Lenin too was a dogmatist, and Stalin too was a revolutionary, just as collective leadership will resort to dogmatism and to revolutionary methods when necessary. What is more, the non-dogmatism of the collective leadership is applied only to itself, to the heads of the new class. On the other hand, the people must be all the more persistently "educated" in the spirit of the dogma, or of Marxism-Leninism. By relaxing its dogmatic severity and exclusiveness, the new class, becoming strengthened economically, has prospects of attaining greater flexibility.

The heroic era of Communism is past. The epoch of its great leaders has ended. The epoch of practical men has set in. The new class has been created. It is at the height of its power and wealth, but it is without new ideas. It has nothing more to tell the people. The only thing that remains is for it to justify itself.

5.

It would not be important to establish the fact that in contemporary Communism a new owning and exploiting class is involved and not merely a temporary dictatorship and an arbitrary bureaucracy, if some anti-Stalinist Communists including Trotsky as well as some Social Democrats had not depicted the ruling stratum as a passing bureaucratic phenomenon because of which this new ideal, classless society, still in its swaddling clothes, must suffer, just as bourgeois society had had to suffer under Cromwell's and Napoleon's despotism.

But the new class is really a new class, with a special composition and special power. By any scientific definition of a class, even the Marxist definition by which some classes are lower than others according to their specific position in production, we conclude that, in the U.S.S.R. and other Communist countries, a new class of owners and exploiters is in existence. The specific characteristic of this new class is its collective ownership. Communist theoreticians affirm, and some even believe, that Communism has arrived at collective ownership.

Collective ownership in various forms has existed in all earlier societies. All ancient Eastern despotisms were based on the pre-eminence of the state's or the king's property. In ancient Egypt after the fifteenth century B.C., arable land passed to private ownership. Before that time only homes and surrounding buildings had been privately owned. State land was handed over for cultivation while state officials administered the land and collected taxes on it. Canals and installations, as well as the most important works, were also state-owned. The state owned everything until it lost its independence in the first century of our era.

This helps to explain the deification of the Pharaohs of Egypt and of the emperors, which one encounters in all the ancient Eastern despotisms. Such ownership also explains the undertaking of gigantic tasks, such as the construction of temples, tombs, and castles of emperors, of canals, roads, and fortifications.

The Roman state treated newly conquered land as state land and owned considerable numbers of slaves. The medieval Church also had collective property.

Capitalism by its very nature was an enemy of collective ownership until the establishment of shareholders' organizations. Capitalism continued to be an enemy of collective ownership, even though it could not do anything against new encroachments by collective ownership and the enlargement of its area of operations.

The Communists did not invent collective ownership as such, but invented its all-encompassing character, more widely extended than in earlier epochs, even more extensive than in Pharaoh's Egypt. That is all that the Communists did.

The ownership of the new class, as well as its character, was formed over a period of time and was subjected to constant change during the process. At first, only a small part of the nation felt the need for all economic powers to be placed in the hands of a political party for the purpose of aiding the industrial transformation. The party, acting as the *avant-garde* of the proletariat and as the "most enlightened power of socialism," pressed for this centralization which could be attained only by a change in ownership. The change was made in fact and in form through nationalization first of large enterprises and then of smaller ones. The abolition of private ownership was a prerequisite for industrialization, and for the beginning of the new class. However, without their special role as administrators over society and as distributors of property, the

Communists could not transform themselves into a new class, nor could a new class be formed and permanently established. Gradually material goods were nationalized, but in fact, through its right to use, enjoy, and distribute these goods, they became the property of a discernible stratum of the party and the bureaucracy gathered around it.

In view of the significance of ownership for its power—and also of the fruits of ownership—the party bureaucracy cannot renounce the extension of its ownership even over small-scale production facilities. Because of its totalitarianism and monopolism, the new class finds itself unavoidably at war with everything which it does not administer or handle, and must deliberately aspire to destroy or conquer it.

Stalin said, on the eve of collectivization, that the question of "who will do what to whom" had been raised, even though the Soviet government was not meeting serious opposition from a politically and economically disunited peasantry. The new class felt insecure as long as there were any other owners except itself. It could not risk sabotage in food supplies or in agricultural raw materials. This was the direct reason for the attack on the peasantry. However, there was a second reason, a class reason: the peasants could be dangerous to the new class in an unstable situation. The new class therefore had to subordinate the peasantry to itself economically and administratively; this was done through the kolkhozes and machine-tractor stations, which required an increase proportionate to the size of the new class in the villages themselves. As a result, bureaucracy mushroomed in the villages too.

The fact that the seizure of property from other classes, especially from small owners, led to decreases in production and to chaos in the economy was of no consequence to the new class. Most important for the new class, as for every owner in history, was the attainment and consolidation of ownership. The class profited from the new property it had acquired even though the nation lost thereby. The collectivization of peasant holdings, which was economically unjustified, was unavoidable if the new class was to be securely installed in its power and its ownership.

Reliable statistics are not available, but all evidence confirms that yields per acre in the U.S.S.R. have not been increased over the yields in Czarist Russia, and that the number of livestock still does not approach the pre-revolutionary figure.

The losses in agricultural yields and in livestock can be calculated, but the losses in manpower, in the millions of peasants who were thrown into labor camps, are incalculable. Collectivization was a frightful and devastating war which resembled an insane undertaking—except for the fact that it was profitable for the new class by assuring its authority.

By various methods, such as nationalization, compulsory co-operation, high taxes, and price inequalities, private ownership was destroyed and transformed into collective ownership. The establishment of the ownership of the new class was evidenced in the changes in the psychology, the way of life, and the material position of its members, depending on the position they held on the hierarchical ladder. Country homes, the best housing, furniture, and similar things were acquired; special quarters and exclusive rest homes were established for the highest bureaucracy, for the elite of the new class. The party secretary and the chief of the secret police in some places not only became the highest authorities but obtained the best housing, automobiles, and similar evidence of privilege. Those beneath them were eligible for comparable privileges, depending upon their position in the hierarchy. The state budgets, "gifts," and the construction and reconstruction executed for the needs of the state and its representatives became the everlasting and inexhaustible sources of benefits to the political bureaucracy.

Only in cases where the new class was not capable of maintaining the ownership it had usurped, or in cases where such ownership was exorbitantly expensive or politically dangerous, the ownership surrendered to other strata or other forms of ownership were devised. For example, collectivization was abandoned in Yugoslavia because the peasants were resisting it and because the steady decrease in production resulting from collectivization held a latent danger for the regime. However, the new class never renounced the right in such cases to seize ownership again or to collectivize. The new class cannot renounce this right, for if it did, it would no longer be totalitarian and monopolistic.

No bureaucracy alone could be so stubborn in its purposes and aims. Only those engaged in new forms of ownership, who tread the road to new forms of production, are capable of being so persistent.

Marx foresaw that after its victory the proletariat would be exposed to danger from the deposed classes and from its own bureaucracy. When the Communists, especially those in Yugoslavia, criticize Stalin's administration and bureaucratic methods, they generally refer to what Marx anticipated. However, what is happening in Communism today has little cönnection with Marx and certainly no connection with this anticipation. Marx was thinking of the danger from an increase in a parasitic bureaucracy, which is also present in contemporary Communism. It never occured to him that today's Communist strong men, who handle material goods on behalf of their own narrow caste's interests rather than for the bureaucracy as a whole, would be the bureaucracy he was thinking of. In this case too, Marx serves as a good excuse for the Communists, whether the extravagant tastes of various strata of the new class or poor administration is under criticism.

Contemporary Communism is not only a party of a certain type, or a bureaucracy which has sprung from monopolistic ownership and excessive state interference in the economy. More than anything else, the essential aspect of contemporary Communism is the new class of owners and exploiters.

6.

No class is established by its own action, even though its ascent is organized and accompanied by a conscious struggle. This holds true for the new class in Communism.

The new class, because it had a weak relationship to the economy and social structure, and of necessity had its origin in a single party, was forced to establish the highest possible organizational structure. Finally it was forced to a deliberate and conscious withdrawal from its earlier tenets. Consequently the new class is more highly organized and more highly class-conscious than any class in recorded history.

This proposition is true only if it is taken relatively; consciousness and organizational structure being taken in relation to the outside world and to other classes, powers, and social forces. No other class in history has been as cohesive and single-minded in defending itself and in controlling that which it holds—collective and monopolistic ownership and totalitarian authority.

On the other hand, the new class is also the most deluded and least conscious of itself. Every private capitalist or feudal lord was conscious of the fact that he belonged to a special discernible social category. He usually believed that this category was destined to make the human race happy, and that without this category chaos and general ruin would ensue. A Communist member of the new class also believes that, without his party, society would regress and founder. But he is not conscious of the fact that he belongs to a new ownership class, for he does not consider himself an owner and does not take into account the special privileges he enjoys. He thinks that he belongs to a group with prescribed ideas, aims, attitudes, and roles. That is all he sees. He cannot see that at the same time he belongs to a special social category: the *ownership* class.

Collective ownership, which acts to reduce the class, at the same time makes it unconscious of its class substance, and each one of the collective owners is deluded in that he thinks he uniquely belongs to a movement which would abolish classes in society.

A comparison of other characteristics of the new class with those of other ownership classes reveals many similarities and many differences. The new class is voracious and insatiable, just as the bourgeoisie was. But it does not have the virtues of frugality and economy that the bourgeoisie had. The new class is as exclusive as the aristocracy but without aristocracy's refinement and proud chivalry.

The new class also has advantages over other classes. Because it is more compact it is better prepared for greater sacrifices and heroic exploits. The individual is completely and totally subordinated to the whole; at least, the prevailing ideal calls for such subordination even when he is out seeking to better himself. The new class is strong enough to carry out material and other ventures that no other class was ever able to do. Since it possesses the nation's goods, the new class is in a position to devote itself religiously to the aims it has set and to direct all the forces of the people to the furtherance of these aims.

The new ownership is not the same as the political government, but is created and aided by that government. The use, enjoyment, and distribution of property is the privilege of the party and the party's top men.

Party members feel that authority, that control over property, brings with it the privileges of this world. Consequently, unscrupulous ambition, duplicity, toadyism, and jealousy inevitably must increase. Careerism and an ever expanding bureaucracy are the incurable diseases of Communism. Because the Communists have transformed themselves into owners, and because the road to power and to material privileges is open only through "devotion" to the party—to the class, to "socialism"—unscrupulous ambition must become one of the main ways of life and one of the main methods for the development of Communism.

In non-Communist systems, the phenomena of careerism and unscrupulous ambition are a sign that it is profitable to be a bureaucrat, or that owners have become parasites, so that the administration of property is left in the hands of employees. In Communism, careerism and unscrupulous ambition testify to the fact that there is an irresistible drive toward ownership and the privileges that accompany the administration of material goods and men.

Membership in other ownership classes is not identical with the ownership of particular property. This is still less the case in the Communist system inasmuch as ownership is collective. To be an owner or a joint owner in the Communist system means that one enters the ranks of the ruling political bureaucracy and nothing else.

In the new class, just as in other classes, some individuals constantly fall by the wayside while others go up the ladder. In private-ownership classes an individual left his property to his descendants. In the new class no one inherits anything except the aspiration to raise himself to a higher rung of the ladder. The new class is actually being created from the lowest and broadest strata of the people, and is in constant motion. Although it is sociologically possible to prescribe who belongs to the new class, it is difficult to do so; for the new class melts into and spills over into the people, into other lower classes, and is constantly changing.

The road to the top is theoretically open to all, just as every one of Napoleon's soldiers carried a marshal's baton in his knapsack. The only thing that is required to get on the road is sincere and complete loyalty to the party or to the new class. Open at the bottom, the new class becomes increasingly and relentlessly narrower at the top. Not only is the desire necessary for the climb; also necessary is the ability to understand and develop doctrines, firmness in struggles against antagonists, exceptional dexterity and cleverness in intra-party struggles, and talent in strengthening the class. Many present themselves, but few are chosen. Although more open in some respects than other classes, the new class is also more exclusive than other classes. Since one of the new class's most important features is monopoly of authority, this exclusiveness is strengthened by bureaucratic hierarchical prejudices.

Nowhere, at any time, has the road been as wide open to the devoted and the loyal as it is in the Communist system. But the ascent to the heights has never at any time been so difficult or required so much sacrifice and so many victims. On the one hand, Communism is open and kind to all; on the other hand, it is exclusive and intolerant even of its its own adherents.

7.

The fact that there is a new ownership class in Communist countries does not explain everything, but it is the most important key to understanding the changes which are periodically taking place in these countries, especially in the U.S.S.R.

It goes without saying that every such change in each separate Communist country and in the Communist system as a whole must be examined separately, in order to determine the extent and significance of the change in the specific circumstances. To do this, however, the system should be understood as a whole to the fullest extent possible.

In connection with current changes in the U.S.S.R. it will be profitable to point out in passing what is occurring in the kolkhozes. The establishment of kolkhozes and the Soviet government policy toward them illustrates clearly the exploiting nature of the new class.

Stalin did not and Khrushchev does not consider kolkhozes as a "logical socialistic" form of ownership. In practice this means that the new class has not succeeded in completely taking over the management of the villages. Through the kolkhozes and the use of the compulsory crop-purchase system, the new class has succeeded in making vassals of the peasants and grabbing a lion's share of the peasants' income, but the new class has not become the only power of the land. Stalin was completely aware of this. Before his death, in *Economic Problems of Socialism in the U.S.S.R.*, Stalin foresaw that the kolkhozes should become state property, which is to say that the bureaucracy should become the real owner. Criticizing Stalin for his excess use of purges, Khrushchev did not however renounce Stalin's views on property in kolkhozes. The appointment by the new regime of 30,000 party workers, mostly to be presidents of kolkhozes, was only one of the measures in line with Stalin's policy.

Just as under Stalin, the new regime, in executing its so-called liberalization policy, is extending the "socialist" ownership of the new class. Decentralization in the economy does not mean a change in ownership, but only gives greater rights to the lower strata of the bureaucracy or of the new class. If the so-called liberalization and decentralization meant anything else, that would be manifest in the political right of at least part of the people to exercise some influence in the management of material goods. At least, the people would have the right to criticize the arbitrariness of the oligarchy. This would lead to the creation of a new political movement, even though it were only a loyal opposition. However, this is not even mentioned, just as democracy in the party is not mentioned. Liberalization and decentralization are in force only for Communists; first for the oligarchy, the leaders of the new class; and second, for those in the lower echelons. This is the new method, inevitable under changing conditions, for the further strengthening and consolidation of monopolistic ownership and totalitarian authority of the new class.

The fact that there is a new owning, monopolistic, and totalitarian class in Communist countries calls for the following conclusion: All changes initiated by the Communist chiefs are dictated first of all by the interests and aspirations of the new class, which, like every social group, lives and reacts, defends itself and advances, with the aim of increasing its power. This does not mean, however, that such changes may not be important for the rest of the people as well. Although the innovations introduced by the new class have not yet materially altered the Communist system, they must not be underestimated. It is necessary to gain insight into the substance of these changes in order to determine their range and significance.

The Communist regime, in common with others, must take into account the mood and movement of the masses. Because of the exclusiveness of the Communist Party and the absence of free public opinion in its ranks, the regime cannot discern the real status of the masses. However, their dissatisfaction does penetrate the consciousness of the top leaders. In spite of its totalitarian management, the new class is not immune to every type of opposition.

Once in power, the Communists have no difficulty in settling their accounts with the bourgeoisie and large-estate owners. The historical development is hostile to them and their property and it is easy to arouse the masses against them. Seizing property from the bourgeoisie and the large-estate owners is quite easy; difficulties arise when seizure of small properties is involved. Having acquired power in the course of earlier expropriations, the Communists can do even this. Relations are rapidly clarified: there are no more old classes and old owners, society is "classless," or on the road to being so, and men have started to live in a new manner.

Under such conditions, demands to return to the old prerevolutionary relations seem unrealistic, if not ridiculous. Material and social bases no longer exist for the maintenance of such relations. The Communists meet such demands as if they were jests.

The new class is most sensitive to demands on the part of the people for a special kind of freedom, not for freedom in general or political freedom. It is especially sensitive to demands for freedom of thought and criticism, within the limits of present conditions and within the limits of "socialism"; not for demands for a return to previous social and ownership relations. This sensitivity originates from the class's special position.

The new class instinctively feels that national goods are, in fact, its property, and that even the terms "socialist," "social," and "state" property denote a general legal fiction. The new class also thinks that any breach of its totalitarian authority might imperil its ownership. Consequently, the new class opposes *any* type of freedom, ostensibly for the purpose of preserving "socialist" ownership. Criticism of the new class's monopolistic administration of property generates the fear of of a possible loss of power. The new class is sensitive to these criticisms and demands depending on the extent to which they expose the manner in which it rules and holds power.

This is an important contradiction. Property is legally considered social and national property. But, in actuality, a single group manages it in its own interest. The discrepancy between legal and actual conditions continuously results in obscure and abnormal social and economic relationships. It also means that the words of the leading group do not correspond to its actions; and that all actions result in strengthening its property holdings and its political position.

This contradiction cannot be resolved without jeopardizing the class's position. Other ruling, property-owning classes could not resolve this contradiction either, unless forcefully deprived of monopoly of power and ownership. Wherever there has been a higher degree of freedom for society as a whole, the ruling classes have been forced, in one way or another, to renounce monopoly of ownership. The reverse is true also: wherever monopoly of ownership has been impossible, freedom, to some degree, has become inevitable.

In Communism, power and ownership are almost always in the same hands, but this fact is concealed under a legal guise. In classical capitalism, the worker had equality with the capitalist before the law, even though the worker was being exploited and the capitalist was doing the exploiting. In Communism, legally, all are equal with respect to material goods. The formal owner is the nation. In reality, because of monopolistic administration, only the narrowest stratum of administrators enjoys the rights of ownership.

Every real demand for freedom in Communism, the kind of demand that hits at the substance of Communism, boils down to a demand for bringing material and property relations into accord with what the law provides.

A demand for freedom—based on the position that capital goods produced by the nation can be managed more efficiently by society than by private monopoly or a private owner, and consequently should actually be in the hands or under control of society exercised through its freely elected representatives—would force the new class either to make concessions to other forces, or to take off the mask and admit its ruling and exploiting characteristics. The type of ownership and exploitation which the new class creates by using its authority and its administrative privileges is such that even the class itself must deny it. Does not the new class emphasize that it uses its authority and administrative functions in the name of the nation as a whole to preserve national property?

This makes the legal position of the new class uncertain and is also the source of the new class's biggest internal difficulties. The contradiction discloses the disharmony between words and actions: While promising to abolish social differences, it must always increase them by acquiring the products of the nation's workshops and granting privileges to its adherents. It must proclaim loudly its dogma that it is fulfilling its historical mission of "final" liberation of mankind from every misery and calamity while it acts in exactly the opposite way.

The contradiction between the new class's real ownership position and its legal position can furnish the basic reason for criticism. This contradiction has within it the ability not only to incite others but also to corrode the class's own ranks, since privileges are actually being enjoyed by only a few. This contradiction, when intensified, holds prospects of real changes in the Communist system, whether the ruling class is in favor of the change or not. The fact that this contradiction is so obvious has been the reason for the changes made by the new class, especially in so-called liberalization and decentralization.

Forced to withdraw and surrender to individual strata, the new class aims at concealing this contradiction and strengthening its own position. Since ownership and authority continue intact, all measures taken by the new class—even those democratically inspired—show a tendency toward strengthening the management of the political bureaucracy. The system turns democratic measures into positive methods for consolidating the position of the ruling classes. Slavery in ancient times in the East inevitably permeated all of society's activities and components, including the family. In the same way, the monopolism and totalitarianism of the ruling class in the Communist system are imposed on all the aspects of social life, even though the political heads are not aiming at this.

Yugoslavia's so-called workers' management and autonomy, conceived at the time of the struggle against Soviet imperialism as a far-reaching democratic measure to deprive the party of the monopoly of administration, has been increasingly relegated to one of the areas of party work. Thus, it is hardly possible to change the present system. The aim of creating a new democracy through this type of administration will not be achieved. Besides, freedom cannot be extended to the largest piece of the pie. Workers' management has not brought about a sharing in profits by those who produce, either on a national level or in local enterprises. This type of administration has increasingly turned into a safe type for the regime. Through various taxes and other means, the regime has appropriated even the share of the profits which the workers believed would be given to them. Only crumbs from the tables and illusions have been left to the workers. Without universal freedom not even workers' management can become free. Clearly, in an unfree society nobody can freely decide anything. The givers have somehow obtained the most value from the gift of freedom they supposedly handed the workers.

This does not mean that the new class cannot make concessions to the people, even though it only considers its own interests. Workers' management, or decentralization, is a concession to the masses. Circumstances may drive the new class, no matter how monopolistic and totalitarian it may be, to retreat before the masses. In 1948, when the conflict took place between Yugoslavia and the U.S.S.R., the Yugoslav leaders were forced to execute some reforms. Even though it might mean a backward step, they set up reforms as soon as they saw themselves in jeopardy. Something similar is happening today in the eastern European countries.

In defending its authority, the ruling class must execute reforms every time it becomes obvious to the people that the class is treating national property as its own. Such reforms are not proclaimed as being what they really are, but rather as part of the "further development of socialism" and "socialist democracy." The groundwork for reforms is laid when the discrepancy mentioned above becomes public. From the historical point of view the new class is forced to fortify its authority and ownership constantly, even though it is running away from the truth. It must constantly demonstrate how it is successfully creating a society of happy people, all of whom enjoy equal rights and have been freed of every type of exploitation. The new class cannot avoid falling continuously into profound internal contradictions; for in spite of its historical origin it is not able to make its ownership lawful, and it cannot renounce ownership without undermining itself. Consequently, it is forced to try to justify its increasing authority, invoking abstract and unreal purposes.

This is a class whose power over men is the most complete known to history. For this reason it is a class with very limited views, views which are false and unsafe. Closely ingrown, and in complete authority, the new class must unrealistically evaluate its own role and that of the people around it.

Having achieved industrialization, the new class can now do nothing more than strengthen its brute force and pillage the people. It ceases to create. Its spiritual heritage is overtaken by darkness.

While the new class accomplished one of its greatest successes in the revolution, its method of control is one of the most shameful pages in human history. Men will marvel at the grandiose ventures it accomplished, and will be ashamed of the means it used to accomplish them.

When the new class leaves the historical scene—and this must happen—there will be less sorrow over its passing than there was for any other class before it. Smothering everything except what suited its ego, it has condemned itself to failure and shameful ruin

The Party State

1.

The mechanism of Communist power is perhaps the simplest which can be conceived, although it leads to the most refined tyranny and the most brutal exploitation. The simplicity of this mechanism originates from the fact that one party alone, the Communist Party, is the backbone of the entire political, economic, and ideological activity. The entire public life is at a standstill or moves ahead, falls behind or turns around according to what happens in the party forums.

Under the Communist systems the people realize quickly what they are and what they are not permitted to do. Laws and regulations do not have an essential importance for them. The actual and unwritten rules concerning the relationship between the government and its subjects do. Regardless of laws, everyone knows that the government is in the hands of the party committees and the secret police. Nowhere is "the directing role" of the party prescribed, but its authority is established in all organizations and sectors. No law provides that the secret police has the right to control citizens, but the police is all-powerful. No law prescribes that the judiciary and prosecutors should be controlled by the secret police and the party committee, but they are. Most people know that this is the case. Everyone knows what can and what cannot be done, and what depends on whom. People adjust to the environment and to actual conditions, turning to party forums or to organs under the party's control in all important matters.

The direction of social organizations and social organs is accomplished simply by this method: the Communists form a unit, which turns to authorized political forums in all matters. This is theoretical; actually it operates in this way: In cases where the social organ or organization is managed by a person who also has power in the party, he will not refer to anyone regarding lesser matters. Communists become familiar with their system and with the relationships created by it; they accustom themselves to distinguish between the important and the unimportant, and refer to party forums only in especially important matters. The unit exists only potentially, important decisions being made by the party; the opinion of those who have elected the government or administration of some organization is totally unimportant.

Communist totalitarianism and the new class took root when the Communist Party was preparing for the revolution; their method of administering and maintaining authority also goes back to that time. The "directing role" in organs of government and social organizations is merely the former Communist unit which has since branched out, developed, and perfected itself. The second "directing role" of the party in the "building of socialism" is nothing but the old theory regarding the *avant-garde* role of the party with respect to the working class, with the difference that the theory then had a different significance for society than it has now. Before the Communists usurped power, this theory was necessary in order to recruit revolutionaries and revolutionary organs; now it justifies the totalitarian control of the new class. One springs from the other, but one is also different from the other. The revolution and its forms were unavoidable and were even needed by that part of society which irresistibly aspired to technical and economic progress.

The totalitarian tyranny and control of the new class, which came into being during the revolution, has become the yoke from under which the blood and sweat of all members of society flow. Particular revolutionary forms were transformed into reactionary ones. This was also the case with the Communist units.

There are two essential methods through which Communist control of the social machine is accomplished. The first is the unit, the main method in principle and in theory. The second, actually more practical one, restricts certain government posts to party members. These jobs, which are essential in any government but especially in a Communist one, include assignments with police, especially the secret police; and the diplomatic and officers corps, especially positions in the information and political services. In the judiciary only top positions have until now been in the hands of Communists. The judiciary, subordinated to the party and police establishments, is generally poorly paid, and is unattractive to Communists. However, the tendency now is for judiciary posts to be considered as a privilege open only to party members, and for members of the judiciary to have increasing privileges. Thus, control over the judiciary could be relaxed, if not completely abolished, with the assurance that it will continue to rule according to the intentions of the party or "in the spirit of socialism."

Only in a Communist state are a number of both specified and unspecified positions reserved for members of the party. The Communist government, although a class structure, is a party government; the Communist army is a party army; and the state is a party state. More precisely, Communists tend to treat the army and the state as their exclusive weapons.

The exclusive, if unwritten, law that only party members can become policemen, officers, diplomats, and hold similar positions, or that only they can exercise actual authority, creates a special privileged group of bureaucrats and simplifies the mechanism of government and administration. In this manner the party unit expanded and more or less took in all these services. As a result, the unit has disappeared while these services have become an essential area for party activity.

There is no fundamental difference in the Communist system between governmental services and party organizations, as in the example of the party and the secret police. The party and the police mingle very closely in their daily functioning; the difference between them is only in the distribution of work.

The entire governmental structure is organized in this manner. Political positions are reserved exclusively for party members. Even in non-political governmental bodies Communists hold the strategic positions or oversee administration. Calling a meeting at the party center or publishing an article is sufficient to cause the entire state and social mechanism to begin functioning. If difficulties occur anywhere, the party and the police very quickly correct the "error."

2.

The particular character of the Communist Party has already been discussed. There are other special features, too, which help reveal the essence of a Communist state.

The Communist Party does not have its unique character solely because it is revolutionary and centralized and observes military discipline and other definite goals, or has other characteristics. There are other parties with similar features, even though these features may be stronger in the Communist Party.

However, only in the Communist Party is "ideological unity" or an identical concept of the world and of the development of society obligatory for its members. This applies only to persons who function in the higher forums of the party. The others, those in lower positions, are obligated only to give lip service to identical ideological views, while they execute orders handed down from above. The tendency, however, is to have those in lower positions adjust their ideological level to that of the leaders.

Lenin did not consider that party members were all obliged to hold the same views. However, in practice, he refuted and explained away every view which did not appear "Marxist" or "the party's"; that is, every view that did not strengthen the party in the manner which he had originally conceived. His settling of accounts with various opposition groups in the party was different from Stalin's, because Lenin did not kill his subjects, "merely" quelled them. While he was in power both freedom of expression and voting privileges were in effect. Total authority over everything had not yet been established.

Stalin required ideological unity—obligatory philosophic and other views—in addition to political unity as a meeting ground for all party members. This is actually Stalin's contribution to Lenin's teaching about the party. Stalin formed the concept of obligatory ideological unity in his early youth: in his time, unanimity became the unwritten requirement of all Communist parties, and it remains so to the present day.

Yugoslav leaders held and still hold the same views. They are still under Soviet "collective leadership" and the forums of other Communist parties. This insistence on the obligatory ideological unity of the party is a sign that no essential changes have occurred, and only confirms the fact that free discussion is not possible, or possible only in a very limited way, under today's "collective leadership."

What does obligatory unity in the party mean and where does it lead?

Its political consequences are very serious. The power in every party, especially in the Communist Party, resides in its leaders and higher forums. Ideological unity as an obligation, especially in the centralized and militarily disciplined Communist Party, inevitably brings with it the power of the central body leadership over the thoughts of its members. Although ideological unity was attained in Lenin's time through discussion held at the top, Stalin himself began to regulate it. Today, post-Stalin "collective leadership" is satisfied to make it impossible for new social ideas to appear. Thus, Marxism has become a theory to be defined exclusively by party leaders. There is no other type of Marxism or Communism today, and the development of another type is hardly possible.

The social consequences of ideological unity have been tragic: Lenin's dictatorship was strict, but Stalin's dictatorship became totalitarian. The abolition of all ideological struggle in the party meant the termination of all freedom in society, since only through the party did the various strata find expression. Intolerance of other ideas and insistence on the presumably exclusive scientific nature of Marxism were the beginning of ideological monopoly by party leadership, which later developed into complete monopoly over society.

Party ideological unity makes independent movements impossible within the Communist system and within society itself. Every action depends on the party, which has total control over society; within it there is not the slightest freedom.

Ideological unity did not arise suddenly but, like everything in Communism, developed gradually, reaching its greatest height during the struggle for power between various party factions. It is not at all accidental that, during Stalin's ascendancy to power in the mid-1920's, it was openly demanded of Trotsky for the first time that he reject all ideas other than those formulated by the party.

Party ideological unity is the spiritual basis of personal dictatorship. Without it personal dictatorship cannot even be imagined. It begets and strengthens the dictatorship, and vice versa. This is understandable; a monopoly over ideas, or obligatory ideological unity, is only a complement and a theoretical mask for personal dictatorship. Although personal dictatorship and ideological unity were already evident in the beginnings of contemporary Communism or Bolshevism, both are firmly establishing themselves with Communism's full power, so that they, as trends and often as prevailing forms, will never again be abandoned until the fall of Communism.

The suppression of ideological differences among the leaders has also abolished fractions and currents, and thus has abolished all democracy in Communist parties. Thus began the period of the *Führer*-principle in Communism: ideologists are merely people with power in the party regardless of inadequate intellectual ability.

The continuance of ideological unity in the party is an unmistakable sign of the maintenance of a personal dictatorship, or the dictatorship of a small number of oligarchs who temporarily work together or maintain a balance of power, as is the case in the U.S.S.R. today. We find a tendency toward ideological unity in other parties also, especially in socialist parties in their earlier stages. However, this is only a *tendency* in these parties; in Communist parties it has become obligatory. One is obliged not only to be a Marxist, but to adopt the type of Marxism desired and prescribed by the leadership. Marxism has been transformed from a free revolutionary ideology into a prescribed dogma. As in ancient Eastern despotism, the top authority interprets and prescribes the dogma, while the emperor is the archpriest.

The obligatory ideological unity of the party, which has passed through various phases and forms, has remained the most essential characteristic of Bolshevik or Communist parties.

If these parties had not at the same time been the beginning of new classes, and if they had not had a special historical role to play, obligatory ideological unity could not have existed in them. Except for the Communist bureaucracy, not a single class or party in modern history has attained complete ideological unity. None had, before, the task of transforming all of society, mostly through political and administrative means. For such a task, a complete, fanatical confidence in the righteousness and nobility of their views is necessary. Such a task calls for exceptional brutal measures against other ideologies and social groups. It also calls for ideological monopoly over society and for absolute unity of the ruling class. Communist parties have needed special ideological solidarity for this reason.

Once ideological unity is established, it operates as powerfully as prejudice. Communists are educated in the idea that ideological unity, or the prescription of ideas from above, is the holy of holies, and that factionalism in the party is the greatest of all crimes.

Complete control of society could not be accomplished without coming to terms with other socialist groups. Ideological unity, too, is only possible through a reconciliation within the party's own ranks. Both the one and the other occur approximately simultaneously; in the minds of the adherents of totalitarianism they appear as "objectively" identical, although the first is a reconciliation of the new class *with its opponents,* and the second is a reconciliation *within the ruling class.* In fact, Stalin knew that Trotsky, Bukharin, Zinoviev, and others were not foreign spies and traitors to the "socialist fatherland." However, since their disagreement with him obviously delayed the establishment of totalitarian control, he had to destroy them. His crimes within the party consist of the fact that he transformed "objective unfriendliness"—the ideological and political differences in the party—into the subjective guilt of groups and individuals, attributing to them crimes which they did not commit.

3.

But this is the inescapable road of every Communist system. The method of establishing totalitarian control, or ideological unity, may be less severe than Stalin's, but the essence is always the same. Even where industrialization is not the form or condition for establishing totalitarian control, as in Czechoslovakia and Hungary, the Communist bureaucracy is inevitably compelled to establish the same forms of authority in underdeveloped countries as those established in the Soviet Union. This does not occur simply because the Soviet Union imposed such forms on these countries as subordinates, but because it is within the very nature of Communist parties themselves and of their ideologies to do so. Party control over society, identification of the government and governmental machinery with the party, and the right to express ideas dependent on the amount of power and the position one holds in the hierarchy; these are the essential and inevitable characteristics of every Communist bureaucracy as soon as it attains power.

The party is the main force of the Communist state and government. It is the motive force of everything. It unites within itself the new class, the government, ownership, and ideas.

For this reason, military dictatorships have not been possible under Communism, although it seems that military conspiracies have occurred in the U.S.S.R. Military dictatorships would not be able to encompass all phases of life, nor even convince the nation temporarily of the need for exceptional efforts and self-sacrifice. Such can be accomplished only by the party, and then only by a party with belief in such vast ideals that its despotism appears to its members and adherents as necessary, as the highest form of state and social organization.

Viewed from the standpoint of freedom, a military dictatorship in a Communist system would denote great progress. It would signify the termination of totalitarian party control, or of a party oligarchy. Theoretically speaking, however, a military dictatorship would be possible only in case of a military defeat or an exceptional political crisis. Even in such a case it would initially be a form of party dictatorship or it would have to conceal itself in the party. But, this would inevitably lead to a change in the entire system.

The totalitarian dictatorship of the Communist Party oligarchy in the Communist system is not the result of momentary political relations, but of a long and complex social progress. A change in it would not mean a change in the form of government in one and the same system, but a change in the system itself, or the beginning of a change. Such a dictatorship is itself the system, its body and soul, its essence.

The Communist government very rapidly becomes a small circle of party leaders. The claim that it is a dictatorship of the proletariat becomes an empty slogan. The process that leads to this develops with the inevitability and uncontrollability of the elements, and the theory that the party is an *avant-garde* of the proletariat only aids the process.

This does not mean that during the battle for power the party is not the leader of the working masses or that it is not working in their interests. But then, the party's role and struggles are stages and forms of its movement toward power. Although its struggle aids the working class, it also strengthens the party, as well as the future power-holders and the embryonic new class. As soon as it attains power, the party controls all power and takes all goods into its hands, professing to be the representative of the interests of the working class and the working people. Except for short periods during the revolutionary battle, the proletariat does not participate or play a greater role in this than any other class.

This does not mean that the proletariat, or some of its strata, are not temporarily interested in keeping the party in power. The peasants supported those who professed the intention to rescue them from hopeless misery through industrialization.

While individual strata of the working classes may temporarily support the party, the government is not theirs nor is their part in the government important for the course of social progress and social relations. In the Communist system nothing is done to aid the working people, particularly the working class, to attain power and rights. It cannot be otherwise.

The classes and masses do not exercise authority, but the

party does so in their name. In every party, including the most democratic, leaders play an important role to the extent that the party's authority becomes the authority of the leaders. The so-called "dictatorship of the proletariat," which is the beginning of and under the best circumstances becomes the authority of the party, inevitably evolves into the dictatorship of the leaders. In a totalitarian government of this type, the dictatorship of the proletariat is a theoretical justification, or ideological mask at best, for the authority of some oligarchs.

Marx envisioned the dictatorship of the proletariat as democracy within and for the benefit of the proletariat; that is, a government in which there are many socialist streams or parties. The only dictatorship of the proletariat, the Paris Commune of 1871, on which Marx based his conclusions, was composed of several parties, among which the Marxist party was neither the smallest nor the most significant. But a dictatorship of the proletariat which would be directly operated by the proletariat is a pure Utopia, since no government can operate without political organizations. Lenin delegated the dictatorship of the proletariat to the authority of one party, his own. Stalin delegated the dictatorship of the proletariat to his own personal authority —to his personal dictatorship in the party and in the state. Since the death of the Communist emperor, his descendants have been fortunate in that through "collective leadership" they could distribute authority among themselves. In any case, the Communist dictatorship of the proletariat is either a Utopian ideal or a function reserved for an elite group of party leaders.

Lenin thought that the Russian soviets, Marx's "ultimate discovery," were the dictatorship of the proletariat. In the beginning, because of their revolutionary initiative and because of the participation of the masses, the soviets did seem to be something of this kind. Trotsky also believed that the soviets were a contemporary political form just as parliaments, born in the struggle against absolute monarchs, have been. However, these were illusions. The soviets were transformed from revolutionary bodies into a form suitable for the totalitarian dictatorship of the new class, or the party.

This was also the case with Lenin's democratic centralism, including both that of the party and of the government. As long as public differences are tolerated in the party, one can still speak of centralism—even though it is not a very democratic form of centralism. When totalitarian authority is created, centralism disappears and the naked despotism of the oligarchy takes over.

We may conclude from this that there is a constant tendency to transform an oligarchic dictatorship into a personal dictatorship. Ideological unity, the inevitable struggle at the top of the party, and the needs of the system as a whole tend toward personal dictatorship. The leader who succeeds in getting to the top, along with his assistants, is the one who succeeds in most logically expressing and protecting the interests of the new class at any given time.

There is a strong trend toward personal dictatorship in other historical situations: for instance, all forces must be subordinated to one idea and one will when industrialization is being pressed or when a nation is at war. But there is a specific and pure Communist reason for personal dictatorship: authority is the basic aim and means of Communism and of every true Communist. The thirst for power is insatiable and irresistible among Communists. Victory in the struggle for power is equal to being raised to a divinity; failure means the deepest mortification and disgrace.

The Communist leaders must also tend to personal extravagance—something which they cannot resist because of human frailty and because of the inherent need of those in power to be recognizable prototypes of brilliance and might.

Careerism, extravagance, and love of power are inevitable, and so is corruption. It is not a matter of the corruption of public servants, for this may occur less frequently than in the state which preceded it. It is a special type of corruption caused by the fact that the government is in the hands of a single political group and is the source of all privileges. "Care of its men" and their placement in lucrative positions, or the distribution of all kinds of privileges, becomes unavoidable. The fact that the government and the party are identical with the state, and practically with the holding of all property, causes the Communist state to be one which corrupts itself, in that it inevitably creates privileges and parasitic functions.

A member of the Yugoslav Communist Party very picturesquely described the atmosphere in which a regular Communist lives: "I am really torn into three parts: I see those who have a better automobile than I have, yet it seems to me that they are not more devoted to the party and to socialism than I am; I look down from the heights on those who have no automobile, for they haven't really earned any. So I'm lucky that I have the one I have."

Obviously, he was not a true Communist, but was one of those who became a Communist because he was an idealist, and then being disillusioned, tried to be satisfied with what might come to him in a normal bureaucratic career. The true Communist is a mixture of a fanatic and an unrestrained power-holder. Only this type makes a true Communist. The others are idealists or careerists.

Since it is based on administration, the Communist system is unavoidably bureaucratic with a strict hierarchical organization. In the Communist system, exclusive groups are established around political leaders and forums. All policy-making is reduced to wrangling in these exclusive groups, in which familiarity and cliquishness flower. The highest group is generally the most intimate. At intimate suppers, on hunts, in conversations between two or three men, matters of state of the most vital importance are decided. Meetings of party forums, conferences of the government and assemblies, serve no purpose but to make declarations and put in an appearance.

They are only convened to confirm what has previously been cooked up in intimate kitchens.

The Communists have a fetishist relation toward the state or the government, exactly as if it were their own property. The same men, the same groups, which are intimate and familiar inside the party become stiff, formal, and pompous individuals when they act as representatives of the state.

This monarchy is anything but enlightened. The monarch himself, the dictator, does not feel himself to be either a monarch or a dictator. When he was called dictator, Stalin ridiculed the idea. He felt that he was the representative of the collective party will. He was right to a degree—since probably no one else in history ever had as much personal power. He, like every other Communist dictator, was aware that a retreat from the ideological bases of the party, from the monopolism of the new class, from ownership of the nation's goods, or from the totalitarian power of the oligarchy, would result in his inevitable downfall. Indeed, no such retreat was even considered by Stalin, as he was the foremost representative and creator of the system. However, even he was dependent on the system created under his administration, or on the opinions of the party oligarchy. He could do nothing against them nor could he pass over them.

The fact emerges that in the Communist system no one is independent, neither those at the top nor the leader himself. They are all dependent on one another and must avoid being separated from their surroundings, prevailing ideas, controls, and interests.

Is there, then, any sense in talking about the dictatorship of the proletariat under Communism?

4.

The Communist theory of the state, a theory worked out in detail by Lenin and supplemented by Stalin and others, favors the totalitarian dictatorship of the party bureaucracy. Two elements are fundamental in the theory: the theory of the state alone and the theory of the withering away of the state. Both of these elements are mutually related and together represent the entire theory. Lenin's theory of the state is most completely presented in his document *The State and Revolution,* which was written while he was hiding from the Provisional Government on the eve of the October Revolution. Like everything else of Lenin's, the theory leans toward the revolutionary aspects of Marxist teaching. In his discussion of the state Lenin developed this aspect further and carried it to extremes, utilizing particularly the experience of the Russian revolution of 1905. Considered historically, Lenin's document was of much greater significance as an ideological weapon of the revolution than it was as a base for development of a new authority built according to its ideas.

Lenin reduced the state to force, or more precisely, to the organ of tyranny which one class employs for the sake of oppressing the other classes. Trying to formulate the nature of the state in the most forceful way, Lenin noted, "The state is a club."

Lenin perceived other functions of the state too. But in these functions he also uncovered what was for him the most indispensable role of the state—the use of brute force by one class against the others.

Lenin's theory calling for the destruction of the old state apparatus was, in fact, far from being a scientific one. This document of Lenin's—extremely significant from the historic point of view—would make valid all that is typical of all Communist theories. In proceeding from immediate needs, the parties create generalities, ostensibly scientific conclusions and theories, and proclaim half-truths as truths. The fact that force and violence are basic characteristics of every state authority, or the fact that individual social and political forces employ the machinery of state, particularly in armed clashes, cannot be denied. However, experience shows that state machinery is necessary to society, or the nation, for still another reason—for the development and uniting of its various functions. Communist theory, as well as that of Lenin, ignores this aspect.

There were, long ago, communities without states and authorities. They were not social communities, but something in transition between the semi-animal and human forms of social life. Even these most primitive communities had some forms of authority. With increasingly complex forms of social life, it would be naïve to try to prove that the need for the state would disappear in the future. Lenin, in support of Marx who agreed with the anarchists about this, contemplated and tried to establish precisely such a stateless society. Without entering into a discussion on the extent to which his premises were justified, we must remember that he contemplated this society as his classless society. According to this theory there will be no classes and no class struggles; there will be no one to oppress and to exploit others; and there will be no need for the state. Until that time, then, the "most democratic" state is the "dictatorship of the proletariat," for the reason that it "abolishes" classes, and by so doing, ostensibly makes itself gradually unnecessary. Therefore, everything that strengthens that dictatorship, or leads to the "abolishing" of classes, is justified, progressive, and liberal. In those places where they are not in control the Communists are pleaders in behalf of the most democratic measures because this facilitates their struggles; in those places where they manage to get control, they become opponents of every democratic form as allegedly a "bourgeois" form. They currently proclaim the preposterous classification of democracy into "bourgeois" and "socialist," although the only proper and fair distinction must be drawn solely on the basis of the quantity of freedom, or the universality of freedom.

In the entire Leninist or Communist theory of the state, there are gaps in the scientific as well as the practical points of view. Experience has demonstrated that the results are completely contrary to those envisaged by Lenin. The classes did not disappear under the "dictatorship of the proletariat," and the "dictatorship of the proletariat" did not begin to wither away. Actually, the creation of the total authority of the Communists, and the liquidation of the *classes of the old society,* was meant to look like the liquidation of *classses in general.* But the growth of state power or, more precisely, of the bureaucracy through which it enforced its tyranny did not stop with the dictatorship of the proletariat. Instead it increased. The theory had to be patched up somehow; Stalin had conceived a still higher "educational" role of the Soviet state before it "withered." If Communist theory of the state, and especially its practice, is reduced to its very essence, i.e., to force and coercion as the principal or only function of the state, Stalin's theory might be said to be that the police system has this high or "educational" role to play. Understandably, only a malicious interpretation could lead to such a conclusion. And in this theory of Stalin's there is one of the Communist half-truths: Stalin did not know how to explain the obvious fact that the power and might of the state machinery continually grew in the already "established socialist society." So he took one of the functions of the state—the educational function—as the main function. He was not able to use tyranny since there no longer were any opposition classes.

The situation is the same with the Yugoslav leaders' theories concerning "autonomy." In the clash with Stalin, they had to "rectify" his "deviations" and do something so that the state would soon begin to "wither away." It did not matter to Stalin or to them that they were further promoting and strengthening that function of the state—force—which for them was the most important function and one on which they based their theory of the state.

Stalin's ideas on how the state withers away while growing stronger, i.e., the way that the state's functions continually expand and draw an ever increasing number of citizens into themselves, is extremely interesting. Perceiving the ever greater and expanding role of the state machine, despite the already "started" transition into a "completely classless" Communist society, Stalin thought that the state would disappear by having all the citizenry rise to the state's level and take charge of its affairs. Lenin, moreover, talked about the time when "even housewives will admininster the government." Theories resembling that of Stalin circulate in Yugoslavia, as we have seen. Neither these nor Stalin's are able to bridge the ever increasing chasm between the Communist theories of the state, with the "disappearance" of classes and the "withering away" of the state in their "socialism" on the one hand, and the realities of the totalitarian authority of the party bureaucracy on the other.

5.

The most important problem for Communism, in theory and practice, is the question of the state; the question is a constant source of difficulties since it is such an obvious contradiction inside Communism.

Communist regimes are a form of latent civil war between the government and the people. The state is not merely an instrument of tyranny; society as well as the executive bodies of the state machine is in a continuous and lively opposition to the oligarchy, which aspires to reduce this opposition by naked force. In practice, the Communists are unable to attain the goal of a state existing solely on naked force, nor are they able to subordinate society completely. But they are able to control the organs of force, that is, the police and party, which in turn control the entire state machine and its functions. The opposition of the organs and functions of the state against the "irrationalities" of the party and police, or of individual political functionaries, is really the opposition of society carried over into the state machine. It is an expression of dissatisfaction because of the oppression and crippling of society's objective aspirations and needs.

In Communist systems, the state and state functions are *not* reduced to organs of oppression, nor are they identical with them. As an organization of national and social life, the state is *subordinated* to these organs of oppression. Communism is unable to solve this incongruity, for the reason that by its own totalitarian despotism it inevitably comes in conflict with dissimilar and opposite tendencies of society, tendencies which are expressed even through the social functions of the state.

Because of this contradiction, and the unavoidable and constant need of the Communists to treat the state predominantly as an instrument of force, the Communist state cannot become a lawful state, or a state in which the judiciary would be independent of the government and in which laws could actually be enforced. The whole Communist system is opposed to such a state. Even if the Communist leaders wished to create a lawful state, they could not do so without imperiling their totalitarian authority.

An independent judiciary and the rule of law would inevitably make it possible for an opposition to appear. For instance, no law in the Communist system opposes the free expression of opinion or the right of organization. Laws in the Communist system guarantee all sorts of rights to citizens, and are based on the principle of an independent judiciary. In practice, there is no such thing.

Freedoms are formally recognized in Communist regimes, but one decisive condition is a prerequisite for exercising them: freedoms must be utilized only in the interest of the system of "socialism," which the Communist leaders represent, or to buttress their rule. This practice, contrary as it is to legal regulations, inevitably had to result in the use of exceptionally severe and unscrupulous methods by police and party bodies.

Legal forms must be protected on the one hand while the monopoly of authority must be insured at the same time.

For the most part, in the Communist system, legislative authority cannot be separated from executive authority. Lenin considered this a perfect solution. Yugoslav leaders also maintain this. In a one-party system, this is one of the sources of despotism and omnipotence in government.

In the same way, it has been impossible in practice to separate police authority from judicial authority. Those who arrest also judge and enforce punishments, The circle is closed: the executive, the legislative, the investigating, the court, and the punishing bodies are one and the same.

Why does the Communist dictatorship have to use laws to the great extent that it does? Why does it have to hide behind legality?

Foreign political propaganda is one of the reasons. Another important one is the fact that the Communist regime must insure and fix the rights of those upon whom it depends—the new class—to maintain itself. Laws are always written from the standpoint of the new class's or party's needs or interests. Officially the laws must be written for all citizens, but citizens enjoy the rights of these laws conditionally, only if they are not "enemies of socialism." Consequently the Communists are constantly concerned that they might be forced to carry out the laws that they have adopted. Therefore, they always leave a loophole or exception which will enable them to evade their laws.

For instance, the Yugoslav legislative authorities stand on the principle that no one can be convicted except for an act which has been exactly formulated by the law. However, most of the political trials are held on the grounds of so-called "hostile propaganda," although this concept is purposely not defined but, instead, left up to the judges or secret police.

For these reasons political trials in Communist regimes are mostly prearranged. The courts have the task of demonstrating what the power-wielders need to have demonstrated; or have the task of giving a *legal* cloak to the *political* judgment on the "hostile activity" of the accused.

In trials conducted by this method the confession of the accused is most important. He himself must acknowledge that he is an enemy. Thus, the thesis is confirmed. Evidence, little as there may be of it, must be replaced by confession of guilt.

The political trials in Yugoslavia are only pocket editions of the Moscow trials. The so-called Moscow trials are the most grotesque and bloody examples of judicial and legal comedies in the Communist system. The majority of other trials are similar insofar as acts and punishments are concerned.

How are political trials handled?

First, upon the suggestion of party functionaries, the party police establish that someone is an "enemy" of existing conditions; that, if nothing else, his views and discussions with close friends represent trouble, at least for the local authorities. The next step is the preparation of the legal removal of the enemy. This is done either through a *provocateur,* who provokes the victim to make "embarrassing statements," to take part in illegal organizing, or to commit similar acts; or it is done through a "stool pigeon" who simply bears witness against the victim according to the wishes of the police. Most of the illegal organizations in Communist regimes are created by the secret police in order to lure opponents into them and to put these opponents in a position where the police can settle accounts with them. The Communist government does not discourage "objectionable" citizens from committing law violations and crimes; in fact it prods them into such violations and crimes.

Stalin generally operated without the courts, using torture extensively. However, even if torture is not used and the courts are used instead, the essence is the same: Communists settle accounts with their opponents not because they have committed crimes, but because they are opponents. It can be said that most political criminals who are punished are innocent from a legal point of view, even though they are opponents of the regime. From the Communist point of view, these opponents are punished by "due process of law," although there may be no legal basis for their being convicted.

When citizens spontaneously turn against the regime's measures, the Communist authorities handle them without regard to constitutional and legal regulations. Modern history has no record of actions against the opposition of the masses which are as brutal, inhuman, and unlawful as those of Communist regimes. The action taken in Poznan is the best known, but not the most brutal. Occupying and colonial powers seldom take such severe measures, even though they are conquerors and accomplish their actions by the use of extraordinary laws and measures. The Communist power-wielders accomplish them in their very "own" country by trampling on their own laws.

Even in non-political matters, the judiciary and the legislative authorities are not safe from the despots. The totalitarian class and its members cannot help but mix into the affairs of the judiciary and the legislative authorities. This is an everyday occurrence.

An article in the March 23, 1955, issue of the Belgrade newspaper *Politika* (*Politics*) offers this suitable illustration of the real role and position of the courts in Yugoslavia (although there has always been a higher degree of legality in Yugoslavia than in other Communist countries):

> In a discussion of problems connected with criminals operating in the economy, at a 2-day annual conference, presided over by public prosecutor Brana Jevremovic, the public prosecutors of the republics, of the Vojvodina, and of Belgrade announced that cooperation between the judiciary organs and the autonomous organs in the economy and all political organizations is necessary for complete success in the battle against criminals operating in the economy and all political organizations....
>
> The public prosecutors think that society has not yet reacted

> with sufficient vigor with regard to ridding itself of such criminals. . . .
>
> The prosecutors agreed that society's reaction must be more effective. According to the thinking of the prosecutors, more severe penalties and more severe methods of executing penalties are only some of the measures that should be taken. . . .
>
> The examples cited in the discussions confirm the opinions that some hostile elements which have lost the battle on the political field have now entered the economic field. Consequently, the problem of the criminal in the economy is not only a legal problem, but also a political one, which requires the cooperation of all government agencies and social organizations. . . .
>
> Summing up the discussion, federal public prosecutor Brana Jevremovic emphasized the significance of legality in conditions resulting from the decentralization that has taken place in Yugoslavia, and pointed out the justification for the severity with which our highest leaders have sentenced individuals guilty of criminal action against the economy.

It is obvious that prosecutors decide that the courts shall judge and that penalties shall be imposed according to the intent of the "highest leaders." What then is left of the courts and of legality?

In the Communist system legal theories change according to circumstances and the needs of the oligarchy. Vishinsky's principle which calls for a sentence to be based on "maximum reliability," that is, on political analysis and need, has been abandoned. Even if more humane or more scientific principles are adopted, the substance will not change until the relationship between the government and the judiciary and the law itself is changed. Periodic campaigns for "legality," and Khrushchev's bragging that the party has "now" succeeded in putting the police and the judiciary under control, only reveal changes in the form of increased needs of the ruling class for legal security. They do not show changes in the ruling class's position toward society, the state, the courts, or the laws.

6.

The Communist legal system cannot free itself of formalism, nor abolish the decisive influence of party units and the police in trials, elections, and similar events. The higher up one goes, the more legality becomes a mere ornament, and the greater the role of government in the judiciary, in elections, and the like becomes.

The emptiness and pomposity of Communist elections is generally well known; if I remember correctly, Attlee wittily called them "a race with one horse." It seems to me that something should be said: Why is it that Communists cannot do without elections, even though they have no effect on political relations; and cannot do without such a costly and empty undertaking as a parliamentary establishment?

Again, propaganda and foreign policy are among the reasons. There is also this: no government, not even a Communist one, can exist without everything being legally constituted. Under contemporary conditions this is done by means of elected representatives. The people must formally confirm everything the Communists do.

Besides this there is a deeper and more important reason for the parliamentary system in Communist states. It is necessary that the top party bureaucracy, or the political core of the new class, approve the measures taken by the government, its supreme body. A Communist government can ignore general public opinion, but every Communist government is bound by the public opinion of the party, and by Communist public opinion. Consequently, even though elections have scarcely any meaning for Communists, the selection of those who will be in the parliament is done very carefully by the top party group. In the selection, account is taken of all circumstances, such as services, role and function in the movement and in society, the professions represented, etc. From the intra-party point of view, elections for leadership are very important: the leaders distribute those party powers in the parliament which they think are most important. Thus the leadership has the legality it needs to operate in the name of the party, class, and people.

Attempts to allow two or more Communists to contend for the same seat in parliament have had no constructive results. There were several instances where this was attempted in Yugoslavia, but the leadership decided that such attempts were "disrupting." News has recently been received of a large number of Communist candidates competing for the same positions in the eastern European countries. The intention may be to have two or more candidates for every office, but there is little possibility that this will be done systematically. It would be a step forward, and might even be the beginning of a turning toward democracy by the Communist system. However, it seems to me that there is still a long way to go before such measures will be realized and that development in eastern Europe will first turn in the direction of the Yugoslav system of "workers' management," instead of becoming a political democracy with its attendant changes. The despotic core still holds everything in its hands, conscious of the fact that relinquishment of its traditional party unity would prove very dangerous. Every freedom within the party imperils not only the authority of the leaders, but totalitarianism itself.

Communist parliaments are not in a position to make decisions on anything important. Selected in advance as they are, flattered that they have been thus selected, representatives do not have the power or the courage to debate even if they wanted to do so. Besides, since their mandate does not depend on the voters, representatives do not feel that they are answerable to them. Communist parliaments are justifiably called "mausoleums" for the representatives who compose them. Their right and role consist of unanimously approving from time to time that which has already been decided for them from the wings. Another type of parliament is not required for this system of government; indeed, the reproach could be made that any other type would be superfluous and too costly.

7.

Founded by force and violence, in constant conflict with its people, the Communist state, even if there are no external reasons, must be militaristic. The cult of force, especially military force, is nowhere so prevalent as in Communist countries. Militarism is the internal basic need of the new class; it is one of the forces which make possible the new class's existence, strength, and privileges.

Under constant pressure to be primarily and, when necessary, exclusively an organ of violence, the Communist state has been a bureaucratic state since the beginning. Maintained by the despotism of a handful of power-wielders, the Communist state wields more power than any other state organization does with the aid of diverse laws and regulations. Soon after its establishment, the Communist state becomes replete with so many regulations that even judges and lawyers have difficulty in finding their way through them. Everything has to be accurately regulated and confirmed, even though little profit is derived thereby. For ideological reasons Communist legislators often issue various laws without taking the real situation and practical possibilities into consideration. Immersed in legal and abstract "socialist" formulas, not subject to criticism or opposition, they compress life into paragraphs, which the assemblies mechanically ratify.

The Communist government is non-bureaucratic, however, where a question of the needs of the oligarchy and the working methods of its leaders is involved. Even in exceptional cases state and party heads do not like to fetter themselves with regulations. Policy-making and the right of political determination are in their hands, and these cannot bear procrastination or too strict formalization. In decisions concerning the economy as a whole and in all other matters except unimportant, representational, and formal questions, the heads function without excessive restrictions. The creators of the most rigid type of bureaucratism and political centralism are not as individuals bureaucrats nor are they bound by legal regulations. For example, Stalin was not a bureaucrat in any respect. Disorder and delay prevail in the offices and establishments of many Communist leaders.

This does not prevent them from temporarily taking a stand "against bureaucratism," that is, against both unscrupulousness and slowness in administration. They are today battling against the Stalinist form of bureaucratic administration. However, they have no intention of eliminating the real, fundamental bureaucratism rampant in the management of the political apparatus inside the economy and state.

In this "battle against bureaucratism," Communist leaders usually refer to Lenin. However, a very careful study of Lenin reveals that he did not foresee that the new system was moving toward political bureaucracy. In the conflict with the bureaucracy inherited partly from the Czar's administration, Lenin attributed most of the difficulties to the fact that "there are no apparatuses composed from a list of Communists or from a list of members of Soviet party schools." The old officials disappeared under Stalin, and Communists from the "list" stepped into their places, and in spite of this, bureaucratism grew. Even in places like Yugoslavia where there was a considerable weakening of bureaucratic administration, its essence, the monopoly of political bureaucracy and the relations resulting from it, was not abolished. Even when it is abolished as an adminstrative method of management, bureaucratism continues to exist as a political-social relation.

The Communist state, or government, is working toward the complete impersonalization of the individual, the nation, and even of its own representatives. It aspires to turn the entire state into a state of functionaries. It aspires to regulate and control, either directly or indirectly, wages, housing conditions, and even intellectual activities. The Communists do not distinguish people as to whether or not they are functionaries—all persons are considered to be functionaries—but by the amount of pay they receive and the number of privileges they enjoy. By means of collectivization, even the peasant gradually becomes a member of the general bureaucratic society.

However, this is the external view. In the Communist system social groups are sharply divided. In spite of such differences and conflicts, though, the Communist society is as a whole more unified than any other. The weakness of the whole lies in its compulsory attitudes and relationships and the conflicting elements of its composition. However, every part is dependent on every other part, just as in a single, huge mechanism.

In a Communist government, or state, just as in an absolute monarchy, the development of human personality is an abstract ideal. In the period of the absolute monarchy, when mercantilists imposed the state upon the economy, the crown itself—for example, Catherine the Great—thought that the government was obliged to re-educate the people. The Communist leaders operate and think in the same way. However, during the time of the absolute monarchy, the government did this in an attempt to subordinate existing ideas to its own. Today, in the Communist system, the government is simultaneously the owner and the ideologist. This does not mean that the human personality has disappeared or that it has been changed into a dull, impersonal cog which rotates in a large, merciless state mechanism, in accordance with the will of an omnipotent sorcerer. Personality, by its own nature both collective and individual, is indestructible, even under the Communist system. Of course it is stifled under this system more than under other systems, and its individuality has to be manifested in a different way.

Its world is a world of petty daily cares. When these cares and wishes collide with the fortress of the system, which holds a monopoly over the material and intellectual life of the people, even this petty world is not free or secure. In the Communist system, insecurity is the way of life for the individual. The state gives him the opportunity to make a living, but on condition that he submit. The personality is torn between what it desires and what it can actually have. It is free to recognize the interests of the collective and to submit to them, just as in every other system; but also it may rebel against the usurping representatives of the collective. Most of the individuals in the Communist system are not opposed to socialism, but opposed to the way in which it is being achieved—this confirms the fact that the Communists are not developing any sort of true socialism. The individual rebels against those limitations which are in the interest of the oligarchy, not against those which are in the interest of society.

Anyone who does not live under these systems has a hard time grasping how human beings, particularly such proud and brave peoples, could have given up their freedom of thought and work to such an extent. The most accurate, though not the most complete, explanation for this situation is the severity and totality of tyranny. But at the root of this situation, there are deeper reasons.

One reason is historical; the people were forced to undergo the loss of freedom in the irresistible drive toward economic change. Another reason is of an intellectual and moral nature. Since industrialization had become a matter of life or death, socialism, or Communism, as its ideal expression, became the ideal and hope, almost to the point of religious obsession among some of the population at large as well as the Communists. In the minds of those who did not belong to the old social classes, a deliberate and organized revolt against the party, or against the government, would have been tantamount to treason against the homeland and the highest ideals.

The most important reason why there was no organized resistance to Communism lies deep in the all-inclusiveness and totalitarianism of the Communist state. It had penetrated into all the pores of society and of the personality—into the vision of the scientists, the inspiration of poets, and the dreams of lovers. To rise against it meant not only to die the death of a desperate individual, but to be branded and excommunicated from society. There is no air or light under the Communist government's iron fist.

Neither of the two main types of opposition groups—that stemming from the older classes and that stemming from original Communism itself—found ways and means of combating this encroachment on their liberty. The first group was tugging backward, while the second group carried on a pointless and thoughtless revolutionary activity, and engaged in quibbling about dogma with the regime. Conditions were not yet ripe for the finding of new roads.

Meanwhile, the people were instinctively suspicious of the new road and resisted every step and small detail. Today, this resistance is the greatest, the most real threat to Communist regimes. The Communist oligarchs no longer know what the masses think or feel. The regimes feel insecure in a sea of deep and dark discontent.

Though history has no record of any other system so sucessful in *checking* its opposition as the Communist dictatorship, none ever has *provoked* such profound and far-reaching discontent. It seems that the more the conscience is crushed and the less the opportunities for establishing an organization exist, the greater the discontent.

Communist totalitarianism leads to total discontent, in which all differences of opinion are gradually lost, except despair and hatred. Spontaneous resistance—the dissatisfaction of millions with the everyday details of life—is the form of resistance that the Communists have not been able to smother. This was confirmed during the Soviet-German war. When the Germans first attacked the U.S.S.R., there seemed to be little desire for resistance among the Russians. However, Hitler soon revealed that his intentions were the destruction of the Russian state and the changing of the Slavs and other Soviet peoples into impersonal slaves of the *Herrenvolk*. From the depths of the people there emerged the traditional, unquenchable love for the homeland. During the entire war Stalin did not mention either the Soviet government or its socialism to the people; he mentioned only one thing—the homeland. And it was worth dying for, in spite of Stalin's socialism.

8.

The Communist regimes have succeeded in solving many problems that had baffled the systems they replaced. They are also succeeding in solving the nationality problem as it existed up to the time they came to power. They have not been able to resolve the conflict of national bourgeoisie completely, however. The problem has reappeared in the Communist regimes in a new and more serious form.

National rule is being established in the U.S.S.R. through a highly developed bureaucracy. In Yugoslavia, however, disputes are arising because of friction between national bureaucracies. Neither the first nor the second case concerns national disputes in the old sense. The Communists are not nationalists; for them, the insistence on nationalism is only a form, just like any other form, through which they strengthen their powers. For this purpose they may even act like vehement chauvinists from time to time. Stalin was a Georgian, but in practice and in propaganda, whenever necessary, he was a rabid Great Russian. Among Stalin's errors, even Khrushchev admitted, was the terrible truth of the extermination of entire peoples. Stalin and Company used the national prejudices of the largest nation—the Russian nation—just as if it had been composed of Hottentots. The Communist leaders will always take recourse to anything they find useful, such as the preaching of equality of rights among the national bureaucracies, which is practically the same to them as the demand for equality of rights among nationalities.

National feelings and national interest, however, do not lie at the basis of the conflict between the Communist national bureaucracies. The motive is quite different: it is supremacy in one's own zone, in the sphere which is under one's administration. The struggle over the reputation and powers of one's own republic does not go much further than a desire to strengthen one's own power. The national Communist state units have no significance other than that they are administrative divisions, on the basis of language. The Communist bureaucrats are vehement local patriots on behalf of their own administrative units, even though they have not been trained for the part on either a linguistic or a national basis. In some purely administrative units in Yugoslavia (the regional councils), chauvinism has been greater than in the national republic governments.

Among the Communists one can encounter both shortsighted bureaucratic chauvinism and a decline of national consciousness, even in the very same people, depending upon opportunities and requirements.

The languages which the Communists speak are hardly the same as those of their own people. The words are the same, but the expressions, the meaning, the inner sense—all of these are their very own.

While they are autarchical with regard to other systems and localistic within their own system, the Communists can be fervent internationalists when it is to their interest to be so. The various nations, each of which once had its own form and color, its own history and hopes, stand virtually still now, gray and languid, beneath the all-powerful, all-knowing, and essentially non-national oligarchies. The Communists did not succeed in exciting or awakening the nations; in this sense they also failed to solve nationality questions. Who knows anything nowadays about Ukrainian writers and political figures? What has happened to that nation, which is the same size as France, and was once the most advanced nation in Russia? You would think that only an amorphous and formless mass of people could remain under this impersonal machine of oppression. However, this is not the case.

Just as personality, various social classes, and ideas still live, so do the nations still live; they function; they struggle against despotism; and they preserve their distinctive features undestroyed. If their consciences and souls are smothered, they are not broken. Though they are under subjugation, they have not yielded. The force activating them today is more than the old or bourgeois nationalism; it is an imperishable desire to be their own masters, and, by their own free development, to attain an increasingly fuller fellowship with the rest of the human race in its eternal existence.

Dogmatism in the Economy

1.

The development of the economy in Communism is not the basis for, but a reflection of, the development of the regime itself from a revolutionary dictatorship to a reactionary despotism. This development, through struggles and disputes, demonstrates how the interference of government in the economy, necessary at first, has gradually turned into a vital, personal interest on the part of the ruling bureaucrats. Initially, the state seizes all means of production in order to control all investments for rapid industrialization. Ultimately, further economic development has come to be guided mainly in the interests of the ruling class.

Other types of owners do not act in an essentially different manner; they are always motivated by some sort of personal interest. However, the thing that distinguishes the new class from other types of owners is that it has in its hands, more or less, all the national resources, and that it is developing its economic power in a deliberate and organized manner. A deliberate system of unification is also used by other classes, such as political and economic organizations. Because there are a number of owners and many forms of property, all in mutual conflict, spontaneity and competition have been preserved in all economies preceding the Communist one, at least under normal or peaceful conditions.

Even the Communist economy has not succeeded in repressing spontaneity, but in contrast to all others, it constantly insists that spontaneity should be achieved.

This practice has its theoretic justification. The Communist leaders really believe that they know economic laws and that they can administer production with scientific accuracy. The truth is that the only thing they know how to do is to seize control of the economy. Their ability to do this, just like their victory in the revolution, has created the illusion in their minds that they succeeded because of their exceptional scientific ability.

Convinced of the accuracy of their theories, they administer the economy largely according to these theories. It is a standard joke that the Communists first equate an economic measure with a Marxist idea and then proceed to carry out the measure. In Yugoslavia, it has been officially declared that planning is conducted according to Marx; but Marx was neither a planner nor a planning expert. In practice, nothing is done according to Marx. However, the claim that planning is conducted according to Marx satisfies people's consciences and is used to justify tyranny and economic domination for "ideal" aims and according to "scientific" discoveries.

Dogmatism in the economy is an inseparable part of the Communist system. However, the forcing of the economy into dogmatic molds is not the outstanding feature of the Communist economic system. In this economy the leaders are masters in "adapting" theory; they depart from theory when it is to their interest to do so.

In addition to being motivated by the historical need for rapid industrialization, the Communist bureaucracy has been compelled to establish a type of economic system designed to insure the perpetuation of its own power. Allegedly for the sake of a classless society and for the abolition of exploitation, it has created a closed economic system, with forms of property which facilitate the party's domination and its monopoly. At first, the Communists had to turn to this "collectivistic" form for objective reasons. Now they continue to strengthen this form—without considering whether or not it is in the interest of the national economy and of further industrialization—for their own sake, for an exclusive Communist class aim. They first administered and controlled the entire economy for so-called ideal goals; later they did it for the purpose of maintaining their absolute control and domination. That is the real reason for such far-reaching and inflexible political measures in the Communist economy.

In an interview in 1956, Tito admitted that there are "socialist elements" in Western economies, but that they are not "deliberately" introduced into the economies as such. This expresses the whole Communist idea: only because "socialism" is established "deliberately"—by organized compulsion—in the economics of their countries must the Communists preserve the despotic method of governing and their own monopoly of ownership.

This attribution of great and even decisive significance to "deliberateness" in the development of the economy and society reveals the compulsory and selfish character of Communist economic policy. Otherwise, why would such an insistence on deliberateness be necessary?

The strong opposition of Communists to all forms of ownership except those which they consider to be socialist indicates, above all, their uncontrollable desires to gain and maintain power. They abandoned or altered this radical attitude, however, when it was against their interest to hold to it; thus they treated their own theory badly. In Yugoslavia, for instance, they first created and then dissolved the kolkhozes in the name of "error-free Marxism" and "socialism." Today they are pursuing a third, and confused, middle-of-the-road line in the same matter. There are similar examples in all Communist countries. However, the abolition of all forms of private ownership *except their own* is their unchanging purpose.

Every political system gives expression to economic forces and attempts to administer them. The Communists cannot attain complete control over production, but they have succeeded in controlling it to such an extent that they continuously subordinate it to their ideological and political goals. In this way, Communism differs from every other political system.

2.

The Communists interpret the special role of those who produce in terms of their total ownership and, even more important, often in terms of the overriding role of ideology in the economy.

Immediately after the revolution, freedom of employment was curtailed in the U.S.S.R. But the need of the regime for rapid industrialization did not bring about complete curtailment of such freedom. This took place only after the victory of the industrial revolution and after the new class had been created. In 1940 a law was passed forbidding freedom of employment and punishing people for quitting their jobs. In this period and after World War II, a form of slave labor developed, namely, the labor camps. Moreover, the borderline between work in the labor camps and work in factories was almost completely eliminated.

Labor camps and various kinds of "voluntary" work activities are only the worst and most extreme forms of compulsory labor. This can be of a temporary character in other systems but under Communism compulsory labor has remained a permanent feature. Although compulsory labor did not take the same form in other Communist countries nor develop there to the extent that it has in the U.S.S.R., none of these countries has completely free employment.

Compulsory labor in the Communist system is the result of monopoly of ownership over all, or almost all, national property. The worker finds himself in the position of having not only to sell his labor; he must sell it under conditions which are beyond his control, since he is unable to seek another, better employer. There is only one employer, the state. The worker has no choice but to accept the employer's terms. The worst and most harmful element in early capitalism from the worker's standpoint—the labor market—has been replaced by the monopoly over labor of the ownership of the new class. This has not made the worker any freer.

In the Communist system the worker is not like the ancient type of slave, not even when he is in compulsory labor camps: the ancient slave was treated both theoretically and practically as an object. Even the greatest mind of antiquity, Aristotle, believed that people were born either freemen or slaves. Though he believed in humane treatment of slaves and advocated the reform of the slavery system, he still regarded slaves as tools of production. In the modern system of technology, it is not possible to deal this way with a worker, because only a literate and interested worker can do the sort of work required. Compulsory labor in the Communist system is quite different from slavery in antiquity or in later history. It is the result of ownership and political relationships, not, or only to a slight extent, the result of the technological level of production.

Since modern technology requires a worker who can dispose of a considerable amount of freedom, it is in latent conflict with compulsory forms of labor, or with the monopoly of ownership and the political totalitarianism of Communism. Under Communism the worker is technically free, but his possibilities to use his freedom are extremely limited. The formal limitation of freedom is not an inherent characteristic of Communism, but it is a phenomenon which occurs under Communism. It is especially apparent with regard to work and the labor force itself.

Labor cannot be free in a society where all material goods are monopolized by one group. The labor force is indirectly the property of that group, although not completely so, since the worker is an individual human being who himself uses up part of his labor. Speaking in the abstract, the labor force, taken as a whole, is a factor in total social production. The new ruling class with its material and political monopoly uses this factor almost to the same extent that it does other national goods and elements of production and treats it the same way, disregarding the human factor.

Dealing with labor as a factor in production, working conditions in various enterprises, or the connection between wages and profits, are of no concern to the bureaucracy. Wages and working conditions are determined in accordance with an abstract concept of labor, or in accordance with individual qualifications, with little or no regard for the actual results of production in the respective enterprises or branches of industry. This is only a general rule; there are exceptions, depending on conditions and requirements. But the system leads inevitably to lack of interest on the part of the actual producers, i.e., the workers. It also leads to low quality of output, a decline in real productivity and technological progress, and deterioration of plant. The Communists are constantly struggling for greater productivity on the part of the individual workers, paying little or no attention to the productivity of the labor force as a whole.

In such a system, efforts to stimulate the worker are inevitable and frequent. The bureaucracy offers all kinds of awards and allowances to counteract lack of interest. But as long as the Communists do not change the system itself, as long as they retain their monopoly of all ownership and all government, they cannot stimulate the individual worker for long, much less stimulate the labor force as a whole.

Elaborate attempts to give the workers a share in the profits have been made in Yugoslavia and are now being contemplated in the East European countries. These quickly result in the retention of "excess profits" in the hands of the bureaucracy who justify this action by saying that they are checking inflation and investing the money wisely. All that remains for the worker are small, nominal sums and the "right" to suggest how they should be invested through the party and trade union organization—through the bureaucracy. Without the right to strike and to decide on who owns what, the workers have not had much chance to obtain a real share of the profits. It has become clear that all these rights are mutually interwoven with various forms of political freedom. They cannot be attained in isolation from each other.

In such a system, free trade union organizations are impossible, and strikes can happen very rarely, such as the explosions of worker dissatisfaction in East Germany in 1954 and in Poznan in 1956.

The Communists explain the enforced absence of strikes by saying that the "working class" is in power and owns the means of production through its state, so that if it did strike, it would be striking against itself. This naïve explanation is based on the fact that in the Communist system the owner of property is not a private individual, but, as we know, camouflaged by the fact that he is collective and formally unidentifiable.

Above all, strikes under the Communist system are impossible because there is only one owner who is in charge of all goods and of the entire labor force. It would be hard to take any effective action against him without the participation of all the workers. A strike of one or more enterprises—supposing that such a thing could happen at all under a total dictatorship—cannot really threaten that owner. His property does not consist of those individual enterprises but of the production machine as a whole. The owner is not harmed by losses in individual enterprises, because the producers, or society as a whole, must make up for such losses. Because of this, strikes are more of a political than an economic problem for the Communists.

While individual strikes are almost impossible, and hopeless as far as potential results are concerned, there are no proper political conditions for general strikes and they can occur only in exceptional situations. Whenever individual strikes have taken place, they have usually changed into general strikes and have taken on a distinctly political character. In addition, Communist regimes constantly divide and disrupt the working class by means of paid functionaries, raised from its ranks, who "educate" it, "uplift it ideologically," and direct it in its daily life.

Trade union organizations and other professional organizations, because of their purpose and function, can only be the appendages of a single owner and potentate—the political oligarchy. Thus, their "main" purpose is the job of "building socialism" or increasing production. Their other functions are to spread illusions and an acquiescent mood among the workers. These organizations have played only one important role—the lifting of the cultural level of the working classes.

Workers' organizations under the Communist system are really "company" or "yellow" organizations of a special kind. The expression "of a special kind" is used here because the employer is at the same time the government and the exponent of the predominant ideology. In other systems those two factors are generally separate from each other, so that the workers, even though unable to rely on either one of them, are at least able to take advantage of the differences and conflicts between them.

It is not accidental that the working class is the main concern of the regime; not for idealistic or humanitarian reasons, but simply because this is the class on which production depends and on which the rise and the very existence of the new class depends.

3.

In spite of the fact that there is no free employment or free workers' organizations, there is a limit to exploitation, even in the Communist system. The search for this limit would require a deeper and more concrete analysis. We will concern ourselves here only with its most important aspects.

In addition to political limits—fear of dissatisfaction among the workers and other considerations which are subject to change—there are also constant limits to exploitation: the forms and degrees of exploitation which become too costly for the system must sooner or later be discontinued.

Thus, by the decree of April 25, 1956, in the U.S.S.R., the condemnation of workers for tardiness or for quitting their jobs was canceled. Also a great many workers were released from labor camps; these were cases in which it was impossible to distinguish between political prisoners and those whom the regime had thrown into labor camps because it needed a labor force. This decree did not result in a completely freed labor force, for considerable limitations still remained in force, but it did represent the most significant progress made after Stalin's death.

Compulsory slave labor brought political difficulties to the regime and also became too costly as soon as advanced technology was introduced in the U.S.S.R. A slave laborer, no matter how little you feed him, costs more than he can produce when you count the administrative apparatus needed to assure his coercion. His labor becomes senseless and must be discontinued. Modern production limits exploitation in other ways. Machinery cannot be operated efficiently by exhausted compulsory labor, and adequate health and cultural conditions have become an indispensable prerequisite.

The limits to exploitation in the Communist system are paralleled by limits to the freedoms of the labor force. These freedoms are determined by the nature of ownership and government. Until ownership and government are changed, the labor force cannot become free and must remain subject to moderate or severe forms of economic and administrative coercion.

Because of its production needs, a Communist regime regulates labor conditions and the status of the labor force. It takes many-sided and all-encompassing social measures: it regulates such things as working hours, vacations, insurance, education, the labor of women and children. Many of these measures are largely nominal; many are also of a progressively harmful character.

In a Communist system the tendency to regulate labor relations and to maintain order and peace in production is constant. The single and collective owner solves labor-force problems on an all-encompassing scale. It cannot support "anarchy" in anything, and certainly not in the labor force. It must regulate it just as much as every other aspect of production.

The great boast that there is full employment in Communist systems cannot hide the wounds which become evident as one looks more closely. As soon as all material goods are controlled by one body, these goods, like manpower needs, must become the subject of planning. Political necessities play an important role in planning and this unavoidably results in the retention of a number of branches of industry, which survive at the expense of others. Thus planning hides actual unemployment. As soon as sectors of the economy can engage in freer play, or as soon as it becomes unnecessary for the regime to sustain and strengthen one branch at the expense of another, unemployment will recur. More extensive ties with the world market can also cause this trend.

Consequently, full employment is not the result of Communist "socialism" but of an economic policy carried out by command; in the final analysis, full employment is the result of disharmony and production inefficiency. It does not reveal the power but the weakness of the economy. Yugoslavia was short of workers until it achieved a satisfactory degree of production efficiency. As soon as it did, there was unemployment. Unemployment would be even higher if Yugoslavia attained maximum production efficiency.

In Communist economies full employment conceals unemployment. The poverty of all conceals the unemployment of some, just as the phenomenal progress of some sectors of the economy conceals the backwardness of others.

By the same token, this type of monopoly ownership and government is able to prevent economic collapse, but incapable of preventing chronic crises. The selfish interests of the new class and the ideological character of the economy make it impossible to maintain a healthy and harmonious system.

4.

Marx was not the first to visualize the economy of future society on a planned basis. But he was the first, or among the first, to recognize that a modern economy unavoidably tends toward planning because, in addition to social reasons, it is being established on the basis of scientific technology. Monopolies were the first to plan on a gigantic national and international scale. Today, planning is a general phenomenon and an important element of the economic policy of most governments, even though it has a different character in industrially developed countries from that in industrially undeveloped ones. Planning becomes necessary when production reaches an advanced stage and when social, international, and other conditions are subject to similar trends. It does not have much connection with anyone's theories, let alone those of Marx, which were constructed on a far lower level of social and economic relations.

When the U.S.S.R. became the first country to embark upon national planning, its leaders, who were Marxists, connected this planning with Marxism. The truth is this: although Marx's teachings were the idealistic basis of the revolution in Russia, his teachings also became the cover for later measures taken by the Soviet leaders.

All of the historical and specific reasons for Soviet planning were attributed to corresponding theories. Marx's theory was the closest and most acceptable because of the social basis and the past of the Communist movement.

Although leaning heavily on Marx in the beginning, Communist planning has a more profound idealistic and material background. How can an economy be administered other than as a planned economy when it has or is going to have a single owner? How could such tremendous investments be made for the purpose of industrializing if they were not planned? Something must be needed before it can become an ideal. So it is with Communist planning. It is dedicated to the development of those branches of the economy which will insure the strengthening of the regime. This is the general rule, although in every Communist country, especially those which become independent of Moscow, there are exceptions to this rule.

Of course, the development of the national economy as a whole is important for the strengthening of the regime, for it is impossible permanently to separate progress in one branch of production from another. Planning emphasis in every Communist system is always directed toward branches of the economy that are considered to be of decisive importance in maintaining the political stability of the regime. These branches are ones that enhance the role, power, and privileges of the bureaucracy. They also are the ones that strengthen the regime in its relations to other countries and make it possible for the regime to industrialize to a greater degree. Up to now, they have been branches of heavy and war industries. This does not mean that the situation cannot change in individual countries.

Recently atomic energy, especially in the U.S.S.R., has begun to take first place in the plan; I should say that this is happening because of military, foreign and political considerations rather than for any other.

Everything is subordinated to these aims. Consequently, many branches of the economy are lagging and working inefficiently; disproportions and difficulties are inevitable; and excessive production costs and chronic inflation are rampant. According to André Philipe (in the *New Leader,* October 1, 1956), investments in heavy industry in the U.S.S.R. increased from the 53.3 per cent of total investments in 1954 to 60 per cent of total investments in 1955. Twenty-one per cent of the net national income is being invested in industry, with a concentration on heavy industry, although heavy industry only contributed 7.4 per cent to the increase in income per capita, 6.4 per cent of which was due to increased production.

It is understandable why, under such conditions, the standard of living is the last concern of the new owners, even though, as Marx himself maintains, men are the most important factor in production. According to Edward Crankshaw, who is close to the British Labour Party, a desperate battle for survival must be fought in the U.S.S.R. by those who earn less than 600 rubles monthly. Harry Schwartz, the *New York Times* expert on the Soviet Union, has estimated that approximately eight million workers earn less than 300 rubles monthly, and the *Tribune,* representing the point of view of the British Labour Party's left wing, adds the comment that this, and not the equality of sexes, is the reason for the large number of women employed at heavy labor. The recent 30-per-cent wage increase in the U.S.S.R. has applied to these low-wage categories.

This is the way it is in the U.S.S.R. It is not much different in other Communist countries, not even in countries like Czechoslovakia which are technologically very advanced. Once an exporter of agricultural products, Yugoslavia now imports them. According to official statistics, the standard of living of blue- and white-collar workers is lower than before World War II, when Yugoslavia was an undeveloped capitalist country.

Communist planning, devoted to political class interests, and totalitarian dictatorship supplement each other. For ideologic reasons, Communists invest intensively in certain branches of the economy. All planning revolves around these branches. This leads to deep displacements in the economy which cannot be paid for by income from nationalized farms taken over from capitalists and large landowners, but must be paid for mainly through the imposition of low wages and the pillaging of peasants through the compulsory crop-purchase system.

It might be said that if the U.S.S.R. had not done such planning, or if it had not concentrated on the development of heavy industry, it would have entered World War II unarmed and would have been the easily conquered slave of the Hitler invasion. This is correct, but only to a certain degree. For guns and tanks are not the only strength of a country. If Stalin had not had imperialistic aims in his foreign policy and tyrannical aims in his internal policy, no grouping of powers would have left his country standing alone before the invader.

This is clear: the ideological approach to planning and development of the economy was not essential for the development of a war industry. It was put into action because of the power-holders' need to be independent internally and externally; defense needs were only associate needs, even though they were inevitable. Russia could have obtained the same quantities of armaments, proceeding under different plans, linking her more closely with foreign markets. Greater dependency on foreign markets would have necessitated a different foreign policy. Under present-day conditions, where world interests are interlaced and where wars are total, butter is almost as important as guns in the waging of war. This was confirmed even in the case of the U.S.S.R. Food from the United States was almost as important for victory as war matériel.

The same is true with regard to agriculture. Under present-day conditions, progressive agriculture also means industrialization. Progressive agriculture does not insure that a Communist regime will be independent of the outside. Internally it makes the regime dependent on the peasant, even though the peasants are members of free cooperatives. Consequently steel has been given priority in the plan, right beside kolkhozes with low production. The planning of political power had to come ahead of economic progress.

Soviet, or Communist, planning is of a special kind. It has not evolved as the result of the technological development of production nor as the result of the "socialist" consciousness of its initiators. Instead it has evolved as the result of a special type of government and ownership. Today, technical and other factors are influencing this type of planning, but these other factors have not ceased to have their effect on the evolution of this type of planning. It is very important to note this, for it is the key to understanding the character of this type of planning, and of the capabilities of a Communist economy.

The results achieved by such an economy and by such planning are varied. The concentration of all means to achieve a specific purpose make it possible for the power-wielders to progress with extraordinary speed in certain branches of the economy. The progress that the U.S.S.R. has achieved in some branches has heretofore never been achieved anywhere in the world. However, when one considers the backward conditions existing in other branches the progress achieved is not justified from the over-all economic point of view.

Of course, once-backward Russia has attained second place in world production as far as its most important branches of the economy are concerned. It has become the mightiest continental power in the world. A strong working class, a wide stratum of technical intelligentsia, and the materials for consumer goods production have been created. The dictatorship has not been essentially weakened because of this, nor are there any reasons to believe that the standard of living cannot be improved in proportion to the country's economic capabilities.

Ownership and political considerations for which the plan is only an implement have made it impossible to weaken the dictatorship to any extent or to raise the standard of living. The exclusive monopoly of a single group, in the economy as well as in politics, planning that is directed toward increasing its power and its interests in the country and throughout the world, continuously postpones the improvement of the standard of living and harmonious development of the economy. The absence of freedom is undoubtedly the final and most important reason for the postponement. In Communist systems freedom has become the main economic and general problem.

5.

The Communist planned economy conceals within itself an anarchy of a special kind. In spite of the fact that it is planned, the Communist economy is perhaps the most wasteful economy in the history of human society. Such claims may seem strange, especially if one has in mind the relatively rapid development of individual branches of the economy, and of the economy as a whole. However, they have a solid basis.

Wastefulness of fantastic proportions was unavoidable even if this had not been a group which considered everything, including the economy, from its own narrow ownership and ideological point of view. How could a single group of this kind administer a complex modern economy effectively and thriftily—an economy which, in spite of the most complete planning, showed varied and often contradictory internal and external tendencies from day to day? The absence of any type of criticism, even of any type of important suggestion, inevitably leads to waste and stagnation.

Because of this political and economic omnipotence, wasteful undertakings cannot be avoided even with the best of intentions. Very little attention is paid to what the cost of these undertakings is to the economy as a whole. How great are the costs to a nation of an agriculture which is stagnant because of the superstitious Communist fear of the peasant and unreasonable investments in heavy industry? What is the cost of capital invested in inefficient industries? What is the cost of a stagnant transportation system? What is the cost of poorly paid workers, who consequently "goldbrick" and work slowly? What is the cost of poor-quality production? There is no counting these costs, nor can they be calculated.

Just as they administer the economy, the Communist leaders handle everything in a way contrary to their own teaching; that is, from their personal viewpoint. The economy is just an area which least tolerates arbitrariness. Even if they wished to do so, the leaders could not take into consideration the interests of the economy as a whole. For political reasons the ruling group determines what is "vitally necessary," "of key importance," or "decisive" in a movement. Nothing stands in the way of its carrying out the matter in question, for the group is not afraid of losing its power or property.

Periodically the leaders indulge in criticism or self-criticism and cite experience when there is evidence that something is not progressing or when tremendous waste has become apparent. Khrushchev criticized Stalin for his agricultural policy. Tito criticized his own regime for excessive capital investments and the waste of billions. Ochab criticized himself for this "conditional" neglect of the standard of living. But the essence remains the same. The same men prolong the same system by about the same method, until breaches and "irregularities" become apparent. Losses incurred can no longer be restored, so the regime and the party do not take the responsibility for the losses. They have "noted" the errors and these errors will be "corrected." So let's begin all over again!

There is no evidence that a single Communist leader has suffered because of unproductively expended or fantastically wasted means. But many have been deposed because of "ideological deviations."

In Communist systems, thefts and misappropriations are inevitable. It is not just poverty that motivates people to steal the "national property"; but the fact that the property does not seem to belong to anyone. All valuables are somehow rendered valueless, thus creating a favorable atmosphere for theft and waste. In 1954, in Yugoslavia alone, over 20,000 cases of theft of "socialist property" were discovered. The Communist leaders handle national property as their own, but at the same time they waste it as if it were somebody else's. Such is the nature of ownership and government of the system.

The greatest waste is not even visible. This is the waste of manpower. The slow, unproductive work of disinterested millions, together with the prevention of all work not considered "socialist," is the calculable, invisible, and gigantic waste which no Communist regime has been able to avoid. Even though they are adherents of Smith's theory that labor creates value, a theory which Marx adopted, these power-wielders pay the least attention to labor and manpower, regarding them as something of very little value which can be readily replaced.

The fear which Communists have of "the renewal of capitalism," or of economic consequences that would arise from narrow class "ideological" motives, has cost the nation tremendous wealth and put a brake on its development. Entire industries are destroyed because the state is not in a position to maintain or develop them; only that which is the state's is considered "socialist."

How far and how long can a nation carry on like this? The moment is approaching when industrialization, which first made Communism inevitable, will through further development make the Communist form of government and ownership superfluous.

The waste is tremendous because of the isolation of Communist economies. Every Communist economy is essentially autarchic. The reasons for this autarchy lie in the character of its government and ownership.

No Communist country—not even Yugoslavia, which was obliged to cooperate to a greater extent with non-Communist countries because of its conflict with Moscow—has been successful in developing foreign trade beyond the traditional exchange of goods. Planned production on a larger scale in cooperation with other countries has not been attained.

Communist planning, among other things, takes very little account of the needs of world markets or of the production in other countries. Partly as a result of this, and partly as a result of ideological and other motives, Communist governments take too little account of natural conditions affecting production. They often construct industrial plants without having sufficient raw materials available for them, and almost never pay attention to the world level of price and production. They produce some products at several times the production cost in other countries. Simultaneously, other branches of industry which could surpass the world average in productivity, or which could produce at lower prices than the world average, are neglected. Entire new industries are being developed, even though world markets are surfeited with the items they will produce. The working people have to pay for all this in order to make the oligarchs "independent."

This is one aspect of the problem common to Communist regimes. Another is the senseless race of the "leading Socialist country"—the U.S.S.R.—to overtake and pass the most highly developed countries. What does this cost? And where does it lead?

Perhaps the U.S.S.R. can overtake some branches of the economy of the most highly developed countries. By infinite waste of manpower, by low wages, and by neglect of the other branches of industry, this may be possible. It is quite another question whether this is economically justifiable.

Such plans are aggressive in themselves. What does the non-Communist world think of the fact that the U.S.S.R. is determined to hold first place in the production of steel and crude oil at the cost of a low standard of living? What is left of "coexistence" and "peace-loving cooperation" if they consist of competition in heavy industry and of very small trade exchanges? What is left of cooperation if the Communist economies develop autarchically, but penetrate the world mostly for ideological reasons?

Such plans and relations waste domestic and world manpower and wealth and are unjustified from every viewpoint except that of the Communist oligarchy. Technical progress and changing vital needs make one branch of the economy important one moment and another the next; this is true for nations and for the world. What will happen if, fifty years from now, steel and petroleum lose the significance they hold today? The Communist leaders take no account of this and many other things.

Efforts at linking the Communist economies, the Soviet first of all, to the rest of the world, and at the penetration of the world by these economies, are far behind the actual technical and other capabilities of these economies. At their present stage these economies could cooperate with the rest of the world to a much greater degree than they actually do. The failure to use their capabilities for cooperation with the outside world and the rush to penetrate the outer world for ideological and other reasons are caused by the monopoly that the Communists hold over the economy and by their need to maintain power.

Lenin was largely right when he stated that politics is a "concentrated economy." This has been reversed in the Communist system; economy has become concentrated politics; that is, politics play an almost decisive role in the economy.

Separation from the world market, or the creation of a "world socialist" market, which Stalin inaugurated and to which Soviet leaders still pledge allegiance, represents perhaps the major reason for world strain and world-wide waste.

Monopoly of ownership, antiquated methods of production—no matter whose or what kind—are in conflict with the world economic needs. Freedom vs. ownership has become a world problem.

The abolishment of private, or capitalist, ownership in the backward Communist states has made possible rapid, if not smooth, economic progress. The states have become uncommonly great physical powers, new and resistant, with a self-righteous and fanatical class which has tasted the fruits of authority and ownership. This development cannot solve any of the questions that were of concern to classic socialism of the nineteenth century, nor even those that were of concern to Lenin; still less can it insure economic advancement without internal difficulties and convulsions.

Despite its powerful concentration of forces in one pair of hands and its rapid if unbalanced successes, the Communist economic system has been showing deep fissures and weaknesses since the moment of its complete victory. Even though it has not yet reached the height of its power it is already running into difficulties. Its future is less and less secure; the Communist economic system will have to battle furiously, inside and outside, for its existence.

Tyranny over the Mind

1.

There is only partial justification for seeking, in Communist philosophy, the sources of tyranny over the mind, a tyranny which the Communists exercise with clinical refinement when they come to power. Communist materialism is possibly more exclusive than any other contemporary view of the world. It pushes its adherents into the position which makes it impossible for them to hold any other viewpoint. If this view were not connected with specific forms of government and ownership, the monstrous methods of oppression and destruction of the human mind could not be explained by the view itself.

Every ideology, every opinion, tries to represent itself as the only true one and complete one. This is innate in man's thinking.

It was not the idea itself but the method by which the idea was applied that distinguished Marx and Engels. They denied every scientific and progressive socialist value in the thinking of their contemporaries, usually lumping such ideas into "bourgeois science," thus banning every serious discussion and study in advance.

The idea that was especially narrow and exclusive with Marx and Engels, the idea from which Communism later could draw substance for its ideological intolerance, was that of the inseparability of the political views of a contemporary scientist, thinker, or artist from his real or scientific value as a thinker or artist. If one was found in the opposite camp politically, his every other objective or other work was opposed or disregarded.

This position of Marx and Engels can be only partially explained as the result of the furious opposition of the owners and power-holders agitated by the "specter of Communism" from the very beginning.

The exclusiveness of Marx and Engels was born and intensified by something else that was at the roots of what they had learned: convinced that they had plumbed the depths of every philosophy, they thought that it was impossible for anyone to attain anything significant without taking their own view of the world as the basis. Out of the scientific atmosphere of the epoch and out of the needs of the socialist movement, Marx and Engels came to think that anything that was not important to them, or to the movement, was not important, even objectively; that is, if it was independent of the movement, it was not important.

Consequently, they proceeded practically unaware of the most important minds of their time, and disdained the views of opponents in their own movement. The writings of Marx and Engels contain no mention of such a well-known philosopher as Schopenhauer or of an aestheticist like Taine. There is no mention of the well-known writers and artists of their period. There is not even any reference to those who were caught up in the ideological and social stream to which Marx and Engels belonged. They settled their accounts with their oppositionists in the socialist movement in a fierce and intolerant manner. This was perhaps not important for the sociology of Proudhon, but it was very important for the development of socialism and social struggles, especially in France. The same may be said of Bakunin. Slaughtering Proudhon's ideas, Marx, in his *Misery of Philosophy,* scornfully went beyond his real role. He and Engels did the same with the German socialist, Lassalle, as well as with other oppositionists inside their own movement.

On the other hand, they carefully noted the significant intellectual phenomena of their time. They accepted Darwin. They particularly grasped the currents of the past—ancient and Renaissance—from which European culture had developed. In sociology they borrowed from English political economy (Smith and Ricardo); in philosophy, from classic German philosophy (Kant, Hegel); and in social theory, from French socialism, or from the currents that emerged after the French revolution. These were the great scientific, intellectual, and social currents that created the democratic and progressive climate of Europe and the rest of the world.

There is logic and consistency in the development of Communism. Marx was more of a scientist, more objective than Lenin, who was above all a great revolutionary, formed under the conditions of Czarist absolutism, semi-colonial Russian capitalism, and world conflicts by monopolists for spheres of influence.

Leaning on Marx, Lenin taught that materialism was progressive as a rule throughout history, and that idealism was reactionary. This was not only one-sided and incorrect, but it intensified Marx's exclusiveness. It also emanated from insufficient knowledge of historical philosophy. In 1909, when Lenin wrote his *Materialism and Empiro-Criticism,* he was not closely acquainted with any great philosopher, classical or modern. Because of the need to overcome oppositionists whose views hindered the development of his party, Lenin rejected everything that was not in accord with Marxist views. To him, anything was erroneous and valueless if it was not in accord with original Marxism. It must be acknowledged that, in this respect, his works are outstanding examples of logical and persuasive dogmatism.

Believing that materialism had always been the ideology of revolutionary and subversive social movements, he drew the one-sided conclusion that materialism was generally progressive—even in the fields of research and in the development of man's thought—while idealism was reactionary. Lenin confused form and method with content and with scientific discovery. The fact that anyone was idealistic in his thinking was sufficient for Lenin to disregard his real value and the value of his discoveries. Lenin extended his political intolerance to practically the entire history of human thought.

By 1920, Bertrand Russell, the British philosopher who welcomed the October Revolution, had accurately noted the essence of Leninist, or Communist, dogmatism:*

> There is, however, another aspect of Bolshevism from which I differ more fundamentally. Bolshevism is not merely a political doctrine; it is also a religion, with elaborate dogmas and inspired scriptures. When Lenin wishes to prove some proposition, he does so, if possible, by quoting texts from Marx and Engels. A full-fledged Communist is not merely a man who believes that land and capital should be held in common, and their produce distributed as nearly equally as possible. He is a man who entertains a number of elaborate and dogmatic beliefs—such as philosophic materialism, for example—which may be true, but are not, to a scientific temper, capable of being known with any certainty. This habit, of militant certainty about objectively doubtful matters, is one from which, since the Renaissance, the world has been gradually emerging, into that temper of constructive and fruitful skepticism which constitutes the scientific outlook. I believe the scientific outlook to be immeasurably important to the human race. If a more just economic system were only attainable by closing men's minds against free inquiry, and plunging them back into the intellectual prison of the middle

* From *Bolshevism: Practice and Theory;* New York, Harcourt, Brace & Howe.

> ages, I should consider the price too high. It cannot be denied that, over any short period of time, dogmatic belief is a help in fighting.

But this was Lenin's period.

Stalin went further; he "devoloped" Lenin, but without having Lenin's knowledge or depth. Careful research would lead to the conclusion that this man, whom Khrushchev himself today acknowledges to have been the "best Marxist" of his time, had not even read Marx's *Das Kapital,* the most important work on Marxism. Practical soul that he was, and supported by his extreme dogmatism, it was not even necessary for him to be acquainted with Marx's economic studies to build his brand of "socialism." Stalin was not closely acquainted with any philosopher. He behaved toward Hegel as he would toward a "dead dog," attributing to him the "reaction of Prussian absolutism to the French revolution."

But Stalin was uncommonly well acquainted with Lenin. He always sought support in him, to a greater extent than Lenin did in Marx. Stalin had considerable knowledge of political history only, especially Russian, and he had an uncommonly good memory.

Stalin really did not need any more than this for his role. Anything that did not coincide with his needs and his views, he simply proclaimed as "hostile" and forbade it.

The three men—Marx, Lenin, and Stalin—are contrasts as men and are contrasts in their methods of expression. In addition to being a revolutionary, Marx was a somewhat simple scientist. His style was picturesque, baroque, unrestrained, and witty in an Olympian sort of way. Lenin seemed to be the incarnation of the revolution itself. His style was flamboyant, incisive, and logical. Stalin thought his power lay in the satisfaction of all human desires, and believed his thinking to be the supreme expression of human thought. His style was colorless and monotonous, but its oversimplified logic and dogmatism were convincing to the conformists and to common people.

It contained simplicities from the writings of the Church fathers, not so much the result of his religious youth as the result of the fact that his was the way of expression under primitive conditions, and of dogmatized Communists.

Stalin's followers do not have even his crude internal cohesiveness nor his dogmatic powers and convictions. Average men in everything, they possess an uncommonly strong sense of reality. Unable to generate new systems or new ideas because of their commitment to vital bureaucratic realities, they are able only to stifle or make impossible the creation of anything new.

Thus is the evolution of the dogmatic and exclusive aspect of Communist ideology. The so-called "further development of Marxism" has led to the strengthening of the new class and the sovereignty not only of a single ideology, but the sovereignty of thought of a single man or group of oligarchs. This has resulted in the intellectual decline and impoverishment of the ideology itself. Along with this, intolerance of other ideas, and even of human thought as such, has increased. The ideology's progress, its elements of truth, have declined in proportion to the increase of physical power of its disciples.

Becoming increasingly one-sided and exclusive, contemporary Communism more and more creates half-truths and tries to justify them. At first sight, it seems as if its views, individually, were true. But it is incurably infected with lies. Its half-truths are exaggerated and debased to the point of perversion; the more rigid and the more inspired it is with lies, the more it strengthens the monopolism of its leaders over society, and thus over Communist theory itself.

2.

The proposition that Marxism is a universal method, a proposition upon which Communists are obliged to stand, must in practice lead to tyranny in all areas of intellectual activity.

What can the unfortunate physicists do, if atoms do not behave according to the Hegelian-Marxist struggle or according to the uniformity of opposites and their development into higher forms? What of the astronomers, if the cosmos is apathetic to Communist dialectics? What of the biologists, if plants do not behave according to the Lysenko-Stalinist theory on harmony and cooperation of classes in a "socialist" society? Because it is not possible for these scientists to lie naturally, they must suffer the consequences of their "heresies." To have their discoveries accepted they must make discoveries "confirming" the formulas of Marxism-Leninism. Scientists are in a constant dilemma as to whether their ideas and discoveries will injure official dogma. They are therefore forced into opportunism and compromises with regard to science.

The same is true of other intellectuals. In many ways contemporary Communism is reminiscent of the exclusiveness of religious sects of the Middle Ages. The observations on Calvinism written by the Serbian poet, Jovan Dučič, in his *Tuge i vedrine* (*Sorrows and Calms*), seem to relate to the intellectual atmosphere in a Communist country:

> . . . And this Calvin, jurist and dogmatician, what he did not burn on the funeral pyre, he hardened in the soul of the people of Geneva. He introduced religious tribulation and pious renunciation in these homes which are even today filled with this cold and darkness; planted a hatred of all merriment and rapture, and damned poetry and music by decree. As a politician and tyrant at the head of the republic, he forged, like shackles, his iron laws over life in the state, and even regulated family feelings. Of all the figures which the Reformation fostered, Calvin is probably the most calloused of the revolutionary figures, and his Bible is the most depressing textbook for living. . . . Calvin was not a new Christian apostle who wished to restore the faith to its pristine purity, simplicity, and sweetness, as it was when it sprung forth from the parabola of Nazareth. This Calvin was the Aryan ascetic, who, severing himself from the regime, also severed himself

> from love, the basic principle of his dogma. He created a people, earnest and full of virtue, but also full of hatred of life and full of disbelief in happiness. There is no harsher religion or more fearful prophet. Of the people of Geneva, Calvin made paralytics forever incapable of any joy. There are no people in the world to whom religion has brought as much tribulation and dreariness. Calvin was an eminent religious writer, as important to the purity of the French language as Luther was important to the purity of the German language, the translator of the Bible. But he was also the creator of a theocracy which was no less like a dictatorship than was the Papal monarchy. While announcing that he was freeing man's spiritual personality, he degraded man's civil personality to the blackest slavery. He confused the people and failed to brighten life in any way. He changed many things, but completed nothing and contributed nothing. Almost 300 years after Calvin, in Geneva, Stendhal observed how young men and young women carried on conversations only about "the pastor" and his last sermon, and how they knew his sermons by heart.

Contemporary Communism also contains some elements of the dogmatic exclusiveness of the Puritans under Cromwell and of the political intolerance of the Jacobins. But there are essential differences. The Puritans rigidly believed in the Bible and the Communists believe in science. Communist power is more complete than that of the Jacobins. Further, the differences emanate from the capabilities; no religion or dictatorship has been able to aspire to such all-around and all-inclusive power as that of the Communist systems.

The conviction of the Communist leaders that they were on the path leading to the creation of absolute happiness and an ideal society grew in proportion to the growth of their power. It has been said in jest that the Communist leaders created a Communist society—for themselves. In fact, they do identify themselves with society and its aspirations. Absolute despotism equates itself with the belief in absolute human happiness, though it is an all-inclusive and universal tyranny.

Progress itself has transformed the Communist power-wielders into boosters of the "human consciousness." Their concern for human consciousness has increased as their power has increased, along with the "building of socialism."

Yugoslavia has not bypassed this evolution. Some of the Yugoslav leaders, too, stressed the "high level of consciousness of our people" during the revolutionary period; that is, while "our people," or some of them, actively supported these leaders. Now, however, the "socialist" consciousness of the same people, according to these leaders, is very low and, consequently, must wait for democracy in order to be raised. Yugoslav leaders openly speak of the fact that they will bestow democracy "when there is growth of socialist consciousness"; a kind of consciousness which they trust will automatically be attained through industrialization. Until then, these theoreticians of a democracy which is doled out in small doses, men who practice something entirely contrary to democracy, maintain that they have the right—in the name of future happiness and freedom—to prevent even the faintest manifestations of ideas or of any consciousness which is unlike theirs.

Perhaps only in the beginning were Soviet leaders forced to maneuver with such shallow promises of democracy "in the future." They now simply maintain that this freedom has already been created in the U.S.S.R. Of course, even they sense that freedom is at work under them. They are constantly "elevating" consciousness; they urge men to "produce"; they cram minds with arid Marxist formulas and the arid political views of the leaders. Worse still, they force men constantly to acknowledge their devotion to socialism and their beliefs in the infallibility and reality of the promises of their leaders.

A citizen in the Communist system lives oppressed by the constant pangs of his conscience, and the fear that he has transgressed. He is always fearful that he will have to demonstrate that he is not an enemy of socialism, just as in the Middle Ages a man constantly had to show his devotion to the Church.

The school system and all social and intellectual activity work toward this type of behavior. From birth to death a man is surrounded by the solicitude of the ruling party, a solicitude for his consciousness and conscience. Journalists, ideologists, paid writers, special schools, approved ruling ideas, and tremendous material means are all enlisted and engaged in this "uplifting of socialism." In the final analysis, all newspapers are official. So are the radio and other similar media.

The results are not great. In no case are they proportionate to the means and measures employed, except for the new class which would, in any case, be convinced. However, considerable results are attained in making it impossible to manifest a consciousness other than the official one, and in combatting opposing opinions.

Even under Communism, men think, for they cannot help but think. What is more, they think differently from the prescribed manner. Their thinking has two faces—one for themselves, their own; the other for the public, the official.

Even in Communist systems, men are not so stupefied by uniform propaganda that it is impossible for them to arrive at the truth or at new ideas. In the intellectual field, however, the plan of the oligarchs results less in production than in stagnation, corruption, and decay.

These oligarchs and soul-savers, these vigilant protectors who see to it that human thought does not drift into "criminal thought" or "anti-socialist lines"; these unscrupulous procurers of the cheap and actually the only available consumer goods—these holders of obsolete, unchangeable, and immutable ideas—have retarded and frozen the intellectual impulses of their people. They have thought up the most antihuman words —"pluck from the human consciousness"—and act according to these words, just as if they were dealing with roots and weeds instead of man's thoughts. By stifling the consciousness of others, and by emasculating human intellect so that it cannot take courage and soar, they themselves become gray, barren of ideas, and completely lacking in the intellectual enthusiasm that disinterested meditation inspires. A theater without an audience: the actors play and go into raptures over themselves. They think as automatically as they eat; their brains cook thoughts in response to the most elementary needs. This is how it is with these high priests who are simultaneously policemen and owners of all the media which the human intellect can use to communicate its thoughts—press, movies, radio, television, books, and the like—as well as of all substance that keeps a human being alive—food and a roof over his head.

Are there not reasons then for comparing contemporary Communism with religious sects?

3.

Nevertheless, every Communist country achieves technical progress, even though of a special kind and in special periods.

Industrialization, rapid as it is, creates a large technical intelligentsia, which, even if it is not especially high in quality, attracts talents and stimulates the inventive intellect. The reasons that help to achieve industrialization rapidly in specific branches of the economy also act as an incentive for inventiveness. The U.S.S.R. has not lagged to any extent in war technology either in World War II or since. The U.S.S.R. is not far behind the United States in the development of atomic energy. Technology is advanced in spite of the fact that a bureaucratic system makes it difficult to adopt innovations; inventions sometimes lie for years in the warehouses of state establishments. The disinterest of producing organizations often deadens inventiveness still more.

Being very practical men, the Communist leaders immediately establish cooperation with technicians and scientists, not paying much attention to their "bourgeois" views. It is clear to the leaders that industrialization cannot be accomplished without the technical intelligentsia, and that this intelligentsia cannot by itself become dangerous. As in every other field, Communists have a simplified and generally half-correct theory with relation to this intelligentsia: some other class always pays the specialists, while they serve it. Consequently, why shouldn't the "proletariat," or the new class, also do this? Acting on this proposition, they immediately develop a system of wages.

In spite of their technical progress, it is a fact that no great modern scientific discovery has been achieved under the Soviet government. In this respect, the U.S.S.R. is probably behind Czarist Russia, where there were epochal scientific discoveries in spite of technical backwardness.

Even though technical reasons make scientific discovery difficult, the main reasons for this difficulty are social. The new class is very interested in seeing that its ideological monopolism is not endangered. Every great scientific discovery is the result of a changed view of the world in the mind of the discoverer. A new view does not fit into the form of the already adopted official philosophy. In the Communist system every scientist must stop short before this fact or risk being proclaimed a "heretic" if his theories do not coincide with the confirmed, prescribed, and desirable dogma.

Work on discoveries is made difficult to an even greater degree by the imposition of the official view that Marxism, or dialectical materialism, is the most effective method for all fields of scientific, intellectual, and other activity. There has not been a single noted scientist in the U.S.S.R. who has not had political trouble. There have been many reasons for this, but one is due to opposition to the official line. There have been fewer occurrences of this kind in Yugoslavia, but conversely, there are instances of the favoring of "devoted" but poor scientists.

Communist systems stimulate technical progress but also hinder every great research activity where undisturbed functioning of the mind is necessary. This may sound contradictory, but it is so.

While Communist systems are only relatively opposed to scientific development, they are absolutely opposed to any intellectual progress and discovery. Based on the exclusiveness of a single philosophy, the systems are expressly anti-philosophic. In such systems, there has not been born, nor can there be born, a single thinker, especially a social thinker—as long as one does not so consider the power-wielders themselves, who are generally also the "main philosophers" and masters for "elevating" the human consciousness. In Communism a new thought, or a new philosophy and social theory, must travel by very indirect roads, generally by the way of literature or some branch of art. The new thought must first hide and conceal itself in order to reach the light and begin to live.

Of all the sciences and all thought, social sciences and the consideration of social problems fare the worst; they scarcely manage to exist. When it is a question of society or of a social problem, everything is interpreted according to Marx and Lenin, or everything is monopolized by the leaders.

History, especially of its own—the Communist—period, does not exist. Imposition of silence and falsification are not only permitted but are general phenomena.

The intellectual inheritance of the people is also being confiscated. The monopolists act as if all history has occurred just to let them make their appearance in the world. They measure the past and everything in it by their own likeness and form, and apply a single measure, dividing all men and phenomena into "progressive" and "reactionary" classifications. In this fashion they raise up monuments. They elevate the pygmies and destroy the great, especially the great of their own time.

Their "single scientific" method is most suitable too in that it alone protects and justifies their exclusive dominance over science and society.

4.

Similar things are happening in art. Here favors are extended, in increasing measure, to already established forms and views of average quality. This is understandable: there is no art without ideas, or without some effect on the consciousness. Monopoly over ideas, the formation of the consciousness, are the prerequisites of the rulers. Communists are traditionalists in art, mostly because of the need to maintain their monopoly over the minds of the people but also because of their ignorance and one-sidedness. Some of them tolerate a kind of democratic freedom in modern art; but this is only an acknowledgment that they do not understand modern art, and therefore believe that they should permit it. Lenin felt this way about the futurism of Mayakovsky.

In spite of this, backward peoples in Communist systems experience a cultural renaissance along with the technical one. Culture becomes more accessible to them, even though it comes largely in the form of propaganda. The new class is interested in the spread of culture because industrialization brings the need for higher-quality work and the need for enlarging intellectual opportunities. The network of schools and professional branches of art has spread very rapidly, sometimes even beyond actual needs and capabilities. Progress in art is undeniable.

After a revolution, before the ruling class has established a complete monopoly, significant works of art are generally created. This was true in the U.S.S.R. prior to the 1930's; it is true today in Yugoslavia. It is as if the revolution had awakened dormant talents, even though despotism, which is also born in the revolution, increasingly stifles art.

The two basic methods of stifling the arts are by opposition toward the intellectual-idealistic aspects of it and by opposition to innovations in form.

In Stalin's time things reached the point where all forms

of artistic expression were forbidden except those that Stalin himself liked. Stalin did not have particularly good taste; he was hard of hearing, and liked octosyllabic and Alexandrine verse. Deutscher has stated that Stalin's style became the national style. The adoption of official views on art forms became as obligatory as the adoption of official ideas.

It has not always been like this in Communist systems, nor is it inevitable that it should be so. In 1925, in the U.S.S.R., a resolution was adopted stating that "the party as a whole can in no way tie devotion to a cause in the field of literary form." By this the party did not renounce its so-called "ideological aid," that is, its ideological and political control over artists. This was the maximum democracy attained by Communism in the field of art. Yugoslav leaders are in the same position today. After 1953, when the abandonment of democratic forms in favor of bureaucracy began, the most primitive and reactionary elements were encouraged; a mad hunt for "petit bourgeois" intellectuals was initiated, which openly aimed at controlling art forms. Overnight, the whole intellectual world turned against the regime. Consequently, the regime had to retract, announcing through one of Kardelj's speeches that the party cannot prescribe form itself, but that it would not allow "anti-socialist ideological contraband," that is, views which the regime considered as being "anti-socialist." The Bolshevik parties had taken this stand in 1925. This constituted the "democratic" limits of the Yugoslav regime toward art. However, the internal attitudes of most of the Yugoslav leaders were far from changed by this. They privately consider the entire intellectual and art world as "insecure," "petit bourgeois," or, putting it mildly, "ideologically confused." Cited in Yugoslavia's greatest newspaper *(Politika,* May 25, 1954) are Tito's "unforgettable" words: "A good textbook is more valuable than any novel." Periodic hysterical onslaughts against 'decadence," "destructive ideas," and "hostile views" in art have continued.

Yugoslav culture, unlike Soviet culture, has at least succeeded in concealing, rather than destroying, dissatisfied and turbulent opinions regarding art forms. This has never been possible for Soviet culture. A sword hangs over Yugoslav culture, but the sword has been driven into the heart of Soviet culture.

Relative freedom of *form,* which the Communists can only periodically suppress, cannot completely free the creative person. Art, even though indirectly, must also express new *ideas* through form itself. Even in Communist systems where art is allowed the greatest freedom, the contradiction between promised free form and compulsory control of ideas remains unresolved. This contradiction crops out from time to time, sometimes in attacks on "contraband" ideas, sometimes in the work of artists because they are forced to use particular forms. It crops out essentially because of conflict between the uncurbed monopolistic aspirations of the regime and the irresistible creative aspirations of the artists. It is, actually, the same conflict which exists between creativeness in science and Communist dogmatism; it has merely been carried over into the field of art.

Any new thought or idea must first be examined in essence, approved or disapproved, and fitted into a harmless frame. As with other conflicts, the Communist leaders cannot resolve this one. But they can, as we have seen, periodically extricate themselves, usually at the expense of real freedom of artistic creation. In Communist systems, it has not been possible, because of this contradiction, to develop genuine subjects for art or to develop art theory.

A work of art, by its very nature, is usually a criticism of a given situation and of given relations. In Communist systems, therefore, artistic creation based on actual subjects is not possible. Only praise of a given situation or criticism of the system's opponents is permitted. Under these terms art can have no value whatever.

In Yugoslavia officials and some artists conplain about the fact that there are no works of art which can show "our socialist reality." In the U.S.S.R., on the other hand, tons of works of art based on actual subjects are created; but since they do not reflect the truth, they do not have any value and are rapidly rejected by the public, later even coming under official criticism.

The method is varied but the final result is the same.

5.

The theory of so-called "Socialist Realism" reigns in all Communist states.

In Yugoslavia this theory has been crushed and is now held only by the most reactionary dogmatists. In this area, as in others, the regime has been strong enough to forestall the development of disagreeable theories but has been too weak to impose its own views. It can be said that the same goes for the other East European countries.

The theory of "Socialist Realism" is not even a complete system. Gorky was the first to use this term, probably inspired by his realist method. His views were that in rude contemporary "socialist" conditions, art must be inspired with new or socialist ideas and must depict reality as faithfully as possible. Everything else that this theory advocates—typicalness, emphasis on ideology, party solidarity, etc.—has either been taken over from other theories or thrown in because of the political needs of the regime.

Not having been evolved into a complete theory, "Socialist Realism" actually means ideological monopolism by Communists. It calls for efforts to clothe the narrow, backward ideas of the leaders in art forms and for their works to be depicted romantically and panegyrically. This has led to a Pharisaic justificaton of the regime's control over ideas and to bureaucratic censorship of the needs of art itself.

The forms of this control vary in different Communist countries, from party-bureaucratic censorship to ideological influence.

Yugoslavia, for instance, has never had censorship. Control is exercised indirectly by this method: in publishing enterprises, artist's associations, periodicals, newspapers, and the like, party members submit everything they consider "suspicious" to the proper authorities. Censorship, or really self-censorship, has sprouted from that very atmosphere. Even though party members may push something or other through, the self-censorship which they and other intellectuals must exercise over themselves forces them to dissemble everything and make unworthy insinuations. But this is considered progress, it is "socialist democracy," instead of bureaucratic despotism.

Neither in the U.S.S.R. nor in other Communist countries does the existence of censorship absolve creating artists from self-censorship. Intellectuals are forced into self-censorship by their status and the reality of social relations. Self-censorship is actually the main form of party ideological control in the Communist system. In the Middle Ages men first had to delve into the thought of the Church on their work; in the same manner, in Communist systems, it is necessary first to imagine what kind of performance is expected and, often, to ascertain the taste of the leaders.

Censorship, or self-censorship, represents itself as being "ideological aid." In the same way, everything in Communism is represented as being devoted to the implementation of absolute happiness. Consequently, the expressions "the people," "the working people," and similar ones—in spite of their vagueness—are used frequently in connection with the arts.

Persecutions, prohibitions, the imposition of forms and ideas, humiliations, and insults; the doctrinaire authority of semi-literate bureaucrats over geniuses; all this is done in the name of the people and for the people. Communist "Socialist Realism" is not different even in terminology from Hitler's National Socialism. A Yugoslav author of Hungarian origin,

Ervin Sinko, has made an interesting comparison of the "art" theoreticians in the two dictatorships:

> Timofeyev, the Soviet theorist, wrote in his *Theory of Literature:* "Literature is an ideology which helps man to get acquainted with life and to realize that he is participating in it."
>
> "Fundamentals of National-Socialist Cultural Policy" states: "An artist cannot be only an artist, he is also always an educator."
>
> Baldur von Schirach, leader of the Hitler Youth, stated: "Every true work of art applies to the entire people."
>
> Zhdanov, member of the Politburo of the Central Committee of the Communist Party of the U.S.S.R., stated: "Everything that is creative is accessible."
>
> In "Fundamentals . . . " Wolfgang Schulz stated: "National-Socialist policy, even that part of it which is called cultural policy, is determined by the Führer and those to whom he has delegated authority."
>
> If we wish to know what National-Socialist cultural policy is, we must look to these men, to what they were doing and to the directives they issued in order to educate responsible associates for themselves.
>
> At the Eighteenth Congress of the Communist Party of the U.S.S.R., Yaroslavsky said: "Comrade Stalin inspires artists; he gives them guiding ideas. . . . The resolutions of the Central Committee of the Soviet Communist Party and the report of A. A. Zhdanov give Soviet writers a completely prepared work program."

Despotisms, even when they are opposing ones, justify themselves in the same way; they cannot even avoid the use of the same words in doing so.

6.

An enemy to thought in the name of science, an enemy to freedom in the name of democracy, the Communist oligarchy cannot but accomplish complete corruption of the mind. Capitalist magnates and feudal lords used to pay artists and scientists as they could and wished, and thus both aided and corrupted them. In Communist systems, corruption is an integral part of state policy.

The Communist system, as a rule, stifles and represses any intellectual activity with which it does not agree; that is, everything that is profound and original. On the other hand, it rewards and encourages, and actually corrupts, all that it thinks will benefit "socialism," that is, the system itself.

Even overlooking such concealed and drastic means of corruptions as "Stalin prizes," the use of personal ties with the powers-that-be, and the capricious demands and purchases of the top bureaucrats—all of which represent extremes of the system—the fact remains that the system itself corrupts intellectuals and, especially, art. Direct rewards from the regime may be abolished, just as censorship may be, but the spirit of corruption and oppression remains.

This spirit is established and stimulated by party-bureaucratic monopolism over materials and mind. The intellectual has nowhere to turn except toward this power, whether for ideas or for profit. Even though this power may not be directly the government's, it extends through all establishments and organizations. In the final analysis it makes the decisions.

It is very important to the artist that restraint and centralism be exercised as little as possible, even though the essence of his social position is not thereby changed. Because of this, it is much easier for him to work and live in Yugoslavia than in the U.S.S.R.

An oppressed human mind is forced to submit to corruption. If one seeks to know why for a quarter of a century there have been scarcely any significant works, especially in literature, in the U.S.S.R., he would find that corruption has played as great or greater a part than oppression in causing this scarcity.

The Communist system persecutes, suspects, and prods into self-criticism its really creative people. It offers its sycophants attractive "working conditions" and lavish honorariums, rewards, villas, vacation centers, discounts, automobiles, ambassadorial mandates, agit-prop protections, and "magnanimous interventions." Thus, as a rule, it favors the untalented, dependènt, and non-inventive. It is understandable that the greatest minds have lost their direction, faith, and power. Suicide, despair, alcoholism, and debauchery, the loss of internal powers and integrity because the artist is forced to lie to himself and others—these are the most frequent phenomena in the Communist system among those who actually wish to, and could create.

7.

It is generally thought that Communist dictatorship practices brutal class discrimination. This is not completely accurate. Historically, class discrimination declines as the revolution slackens off, but ideological discrimination increases. The illusion that the proletariat is in power is inaccurate; so, too, is the proposition that Communists persecute someone because he is a bourgeois. Their measures do aim most harshly at the members of the ruling classes, especially the bourgeoisie. But those bourgeois who capitulate, or reorient themselves, are able to assure for themselves lucrative posts and favor. What is more, the secret police often find able agents in their ranks, while the new power-wielders find them able servants. Only those who do not ideologically approve the Communist measures and views are punished without consideration as to their class or their attitude toward nationalization of capitalist property.

Persecution of democratic and socialist thought which is at variance with that of the ruling oligarchy is fiercer and more complete than persecution of the most reactionary followers of the former regime. This is understandable: the last named are less dangerous since they look to a past which has little likelihood of returning and reconquering.

Whenever Communists come to power, their assault on private ownership creates the illusion that their measures are primarily directed against the ownership classes for the benefit of the working class. Subsequent events prove that their measures were not taken for this purpose but in order to establish their own ownership. This must manifest itself predominantly as ideological rather than class discrimination. If this were not true, if they really strove for actual ownership by the working masses, then class discrimination actually would have prevailed.

The fact that ideological discrimination prevails leads, at first sight, to the conclusion that a new religious sect has risen, a sect which rigidly sticks to its materialistic and atheistic prescriptions and forcibly imposes them on others. Communists do behave like a religious sect even though they are not really one.

This totalitarian ideology is not only the result of certain forms of government and of ownership. For its part, the ideology aided in their creation and supports them in every way. Ideological discrimination is a condition for the continuance of the Communist system.

It would be wrong to think that other forms of discrimination—race, caste, national—are worse than ideological discrimination. They may seem more brutal to all outward appearances, but they are not as refined or complete. They aim at the activities of society, while ideological discrimination aims at society as a whole, and at every individual. Other types of discrimination may crush a human being physically, while ideological discrimination strikes at the very thing in the human being which is perhaps most peculiarly his own. Tyranny over the mind is the most complete and most brutal type of tyranny; every other tyranny begins and ends with it.

On the one hand the ideological discrimination in Communist systems aims at prohibiting other ideas; on the other, at imposing exclusively its own ideas. These are two most striking forms of unbelievable, total tyranny.

Thought is the most creative force. It uncovers what is new. Men can neither live nor produce if they do not think or contemplate. Even though they may deny it, Communists are forced to accept this fact in practice. Thus they make it impossible for any thought other than their own to prevail.

Man may renounce much. But he must think and he has a deep need to express his thoughts. It is profoundly sickening to be compelled to remain silent when there is need for expression. It is tyranny at its worst to compel men not to think as they do, to compel men to express thoughts that are not their own.

The limitation of freedom of thought is not only an attack on specific political and social rights, but an attack on the human being as such. Man's imperishable aspirations for freedom of thought always emerge in concrete from. If they have not yet become apparent in Communist systems, this does not mean that they do not exist. Today they lie in dark and apathetic resistance, and in the unshapen hopes of the people. It is as if totality of oppression were erasing differences in national strata, uniting all people in the demand for freedom of thought and for freedom in general.

History will pardon Communists for much, establishing that they were forced into many brutal acts because of circumstances and the need to defend their existence. But the stifling of every divergent thought, the exclusive monopoly over thinking for the purpose of defending their personal interests, will nail the Communists to a cross of shame in history.

The Aim and The Means

1.

All revolutions and all revolutionaries use oppressive and unscrupulous means in abundance.

However, earlier revolutionaries were not as conscious of their methods as the Communists have been. They were unable to adapt and use their methods to the degree that the Communists have done.

"You don't need to pick and choose the means to use against enemies of the movement. . . . You must punish not only the traitors, but also the indifferent; you must punish all who are inactive in the republic, all who do nothing for it."

These words of Saint-Just might have been uttered by some Communist leader of today. But Saint-Just flung them out in the heat of the revolution, to preserve its destiny. The Communists speak these words and act according to them constantly—from the beginning of their revolution until they reach complete power, and even in their decline.

Although Communist methods surpass any of those of other revolutionaries in range, duration, and severity, during a revolution the Communists have not as a rule used all the means that their antagonists used. However, even though the methods of the Communists might have been less bloody, they became increasingly more inhumane the farther away they got from the revolution.

Like every social and political movement, Communism must use methods primarily suited to the interests and relations of the powers-that-be. Other considerations, including moral ones, are subordinated.

Here, we are interested only in the methods used by contemporary Communism, which may, according to conditions, be mild or severe, human or inhuman, but which are different from those used by other political and social movements and distinguish Communism from other movements, revolutionary or not.

This distinction does not lie in the fact that Communist methods are perhaps the most brutal ones recorded in history. It is true that brutality is their most obvious but not their most intrinsic aspect. A movement which had as its aim the transformation of the economy and of society by means of tyranny had to resort to brutal methods. But all other revolutionary movements had and wanted to use the same methods. Yet, the fact that their tyranny was of shorter duration was the reason that they could not use all these methods. In addition, their oppression could not be as total as that of the Communists, because it came about under circumstances which did not permit it to be as total.

It would be even less justifiable to seek the reasons for Communist methods in the fact that Communists lack ethical or moral principles. Except for the fact that they are Communists, they are men like all others who in relationships among themselves abide by the moral principles customary in human societies. Lack of ethics among them is not the reason for their methods but the result of them. In principles and in words, Communists subscribe to ethical precepts and humane methods. They belive that they are "temporarily" forced to resort to something contrary to their ethical views. Communists too think that it would be much better if they did not have to act contrary to their ethical views. In this they are not much different from participants in other political movements, except that they have divorced themselves from humanity in a more permanent and monstrous form.

Numerous features which distinguish contemporary Communism from other movements in the use of methods can be found. These features are predominantly quantitative or are actuated by varied historical conditions and by the aims of Communists.

However, there is an integral feature of contemporary Communism which distinguishes its methods from those of other political movements. At first sight this feature might seem similar to features of some churches in the past. It stems from the idealistic aims which the Communists will use any means to further. These means have become increasingly reckless as the aims became unrealizable. The use of their methods, even for the attainment of idealistic aims, cannot be justified by any moral principle. Their use brands those who use them as unscrupulous and merciless power-wielders. The former classes, parties, and forms of ownership no longer exist or have been incapacitated, yet methods have not been changed essentially. Indeed, these methods are just now achieving their full measure of inhumanity.

As the new exploiting class climbs to power, it tries to justify its non-idealistic methods by invoking its idealistic aims. The inhumanity of Stalin's methods reached its greatest height when he built a "socialist society." Because the new class must show that its interests are exclusively and ideally the aim of society and because it must maintain intellectual and every other type of monopoly, the new class must proclaim that the methods it uses are not important. The end is important, shout its representatives, everything else is trifling. What is important is that we now "have" socialism. So do the Communists justify tyranny, baseness, and crime.

Of course, the end must be assured by special instruments—

by the party. It becomes something dominant and supreme unto itself, like the Church in the Middle Ages. To quote Dietrich von Nieheim, nominal Bishop of Verden, writing in 1411:

"When its existence is threatened, the church is freed of moral edicts. Unity as an aim blesses all means: perfidy, treachery, tyranny, simony, prisons, and death. For every holy order exists because of the aims of society, and personality must be sacrificed to the general good."

These words, too, sound as if they had been uttered by some contemporary Communist.

There is much of the feudal and fanatic in the dogmatism of contemporary Communism. But neither are we living in the Middle Ages nor is contemporary Communism a church. The emphasis on ideological and other monopolism only seems to make contemporary Communism similar to the medieval Church; the essence of each is different. The Church was only partly owner and governor; in the most extreme cases, it aspired to perpetuate a given social system through absolute control of the mind. The churches persecuted heretics, even for dogmatic reasons which were not always called for by direct practical needs. As the Church represented it, it was attempting to save sinful, heretical souls by destroying their bodies. All earthly means were considered permissible for the purpose of attaining the heavenly kingdom.

But the Communists first of all desire physical or state authority. Intellectual control and persecution exercised for dogmatic reasons are only auxiliary aids for strengthening the power of the state. Unlike the Church, Communism is not the support of the system but its embodiment.

The new class did not arise suddenly, but was developed from a revolutionary to an ownership and reactionary group. Its methods too, even though they seemed the same, changed in essence from revolutionary ones to tyrannical ones, from protective to despotic ones.

Communist methods will in essence be amoral and unscrupulous, even, when they are especially severe in form. Because it is completely totalitarian, Communist rule cannot allow for much choice of means. And Communists are incapable of renouncing the essential thing—the lack of choice of means—because of the fact that they want to retain absolute power and their own egotistical interests.

Even if they did not so wish, Communists must be both owners and despots and must utilize many means for that purpose. In spite of any happy theories or good inclinations they might have, the system itself drives them to the utilization of any means. In case of any urgency, they find themselves the moral and intellectual champions and the actual users of any means available.

2.

Communists speak of "Communist morale," "the new Socialist man," and similar concepts as if they were speaking of some higher ethical categories. These hazy concepts have only one practical meaning—the cementing of Communist ranks and opposition to foreign influence. As actual ethical categories, however, they do not exist.

Since no special Communist ethics nor a Socialist Man can emerge, the caste spirit of the Communists, and special moral and other concepts, which they nurse among themselves, are are all the more strongly developed. These are not absolute principles, but changing moral standards. They are embedded in the Communist hierarchical system in which almost anything is permitted at the top—the upper circles—while the same things are condemned if they are practiced at lower echelons—the lower circles.

This caste spirit and these morals, changeable and incomplete, have undergone a long and varied development, and have even often been the stimulus for the further development of the new class. The end result of this development has been the creation of special sets of moral standards for various castes, always subordinated to the practical needs of the oligarchy. The formation of these caste morals roughly corresponds to the rise of the new class and is identical with its abandonment of humane, really ethical standards.

These propositions require detailed exposition.

Like all other aspects of Communism, caste morals developed from revolutionary morals. At first, in spite of the fact that they were a part of an isolated movement, these morals were proclaimed as being more humane than those of any sect or caste. But a Communist movement always begins as one of highest idealism and most selfless sacrifice, attracting into its ranks the most gifted, the bravest, and even the most noble intellects of the nation.

This statement, just as most of the others made here, relates to countries in which Communism has developed for the most part because of national conditions, and where it has attained full power (Russia, Yugoslavia, and China). However, with some modifications this statement also applies to Communism in other countries.

Everywhere, Communism begins as an aspiration toward a beautiful ideal society. As such, it attracts and inspires men of high moral standards and of other high distinction. But since Communism is also an international movement, it turns, like a sunflower to the sun, to the movement which is strongest —until now primarily in the U.S.S.R. Consequently, even the Communists of other countries where they are not in power rapidly lose the features they had in the beginning and take on those of the power-wielding Communism. As a result, the Communist leaders in the West, and in other places, have accustomed themselves to play as easily with the truth and ethical principles as the Communists in the U.S.S.R. Every Communist movement at first also has high moral features which isolated individuals may retain even longer and which provoke crises when leaders initiate amoral proceedings and arbitrary turn-abouts.

History does not have many movements that, like Communism, began their climb with such high moral prinicples and with such devoted, enthusiastic, and clever fighters, attached to each other not only by ideas and suffering, but also by selfless love, comradeship, solidarity, and that warm and direct sincerity that can be produced only by battles in which men are doomed either to win or die. Cooperative efforts, thoughts, and desires; even the most intense effort to attain the same method of thinking and feeling, the finding of personal happiness and the building of individuality through complete devotion to the party and workers' collective; enthusiastic sacrificing for others; care and protection for the young, and tender respect for the old—these are the ideals of true Communists when the movement is in its inception and still truly Communist.

Communist woman too is more than a comrade or co-fighter. It can never be forgotten that she, on entering the movement, decided to sacrifice all—the happiness of both love and of motherhood. Between men and women in the movement, a clean, modest and warm relationship is fostered: a relationship in which comradely care has become sexless passion. Loyalty, mutual aid, frankness about even the most intimate thoughts—these are generally the ideals of true, ideal Communists.

This is true only while the movement is young, before it has tasted the fruits of power.

The road to the attainment of these ideals is very long and difficult. Communists and Communist movements are formed from varied social forces and centers. Internal homogeneity is not attained overnight, but through the fierce battles of varied groups and fractions. If conditions are favorable, the group or fraction which wins the battle is the one which has been most aware of the advance toward Communism and which, when taking over power, is also the most moral. Through moral crises, through political intrigues and insinuations, mutual calumniation, unreasoning hatred and barbaric encounters, through debauchery and intellectual decadence, the movement slowly climbs, crushing groups and individuals, discarding the superfluous, forging its core and its dogma, its morals and psychology, atmosphere, and manner of work.

When it becomes truly revolutionary, the Communist movement and its followers achieve, for a moment, the high moral standards described here. This is a moment in Communism when it is difficult to separate words from deeds, or more accurately, when the leading, most important, truest, and ideal Communists sincerely believe in their ideals and aspire to put them into practice in their methods and in their personal life. This is the moment on the eve of the battle for power, a moment which occurs only in movements which arrive at this unique point.

True, these are the morals of a sect, but they are morals on a high plane. The movement is isolated, it often does not see the truth, but this does not mean that the movement does not therefore aim at, or that it does not love, truth.

Internal moral and intellectual fusion are the result of a long battle for ideological and operational unity. Without this fusion there cannot even be any thought of a true revolutionary Communist movement. "Unity of mind and action" is impossible without psychic-moral unity. And vice versa. But this very psychic and moral unity—for which no statutes or laws have been written, but which occurs spontaneously, to become a custom and a conscious habit—more than anything else makes Communists that indestructible family, incomprehensible and impenetrable to others, inflexible in the solidarity and identity of its reactions, thoughts, and feelings. More than anything else, the existence of this psychic-moral unity—which is not attained all at once and which is not even finally formed except as something to aspire to—is the most reliable sign that the Communist movement has established itself and has become irresistible to its followers and to many others, powerful because it is fused into one piece, one soul, and one body. This is the proof that a new, homogeneous movement has emerged, a movement facing a future completely different from the future which the movement foresaw at the beginning.

However, all this slowly fades, disintegrates, and drowns during the course of the climb to complete power and to ownership by the Communists. Only the bare forms and observances which have no real substance remain.

The internal monolithic cohesion which was created in the struggle with the oppositionists and with the half-Communist groups is transformed into a unity of obedient counselors and robot-bureaucrats inside the movement. During the climb to power, intolerance, servility, incomplete thinking, control of personal life—which once was comradely aid but is now a form of oligarchic management—hierarchical rigidity and introversion, the nominal and neglected role of women, opportunism, self-centeredness, and outrage repress the once-existent high principles. The wonderful human characteristics of an isolated movement are slowly transformed into the intolerant and Pharisaical morals of a privileged caste. Thus, politicking and servility replace the former straightforwardness of the revolution. Where the former heroes who were ready to sacrifice everything, including life, for others and for an idea, for the good of the people, have not been killed or pushed aside, they become self-centered cowards without ideas or comrades, willing to renounce everything—honor, name, truth, and morals—in order to keep their place in the ruling class and the hierachical circle. The world has seen few heroes as ready to sacrifice and suffer as the Communists were on the eve of and during the revolution. It has probably never seen such characterless wretches and stupid defenders of arid formulas as they become after attaining power. Wonderful human features were the condition for creating and attracting power for the movement; exclusive caste spirit and complete lack of ethical principles and virtues have become conditions for the power and maintenance of the movement. Honor, sincerity, sacrific, and love of the truth were once things that could be understood for their own sakes; now, deliberate lies, sycophancy, slander, deception, and provocation gradually become the inevitable attendants of the dark, intolerant, and all-inclusive might of the new class, and even affect relations between the members of the class.

3.

Whoever has not grasped this dialectic of the development of Communism has not been able to understand the so-called Moscow trials. Nor can he understand why the Communists' periodic moral crises, caused by the abandonment of the sacred and consecrated principles of the day before yesterday, cannot have the great significance that such crises have for ordinary people or other movements.

Khrushchev acknowledged that truncheons played the main role in the "confessions" and the self-condemnation of Stalin's purges. He claimed that drugs were not used, although there is evidence that they were. But the most potent drugs for forcing "confessions" were in the make-up of the criminal himself.

Common criminals, that is, those who are not Communists, do not go into trances and make hysterical confessions and pray for death as a reward for their "sins." This was done only by "men of a special stamp"—the Communists. They were first morally shocked by the violence and amorality of the beatings and accusations leveled at them secretly by the top party leadership, in whose complete amorality they could not believe, even if they had occasionally found fault with them before. Suddenly, they found themselves uprooted; their own class in the person of Communist leadership had left them; innocent as they were, the class itself had even nailed them to the cross as criminals and traitors. Long ago they had been educated to believe and had proclaimed that they were connected in every fiber of their being to the party and its ideals. Now, uprooted, they found themselves completely bereft. They either did not know or had forgotten or renounced all of those outside the Communist sect and its narrow ideas. Now it was too late to get acquainted with anything but Communism. They were entirely alone.

Man cannot fight or live outside of society. This is his immutable characteristic, one which Aristotle noted and explained, calling it "political being."

What else is left to a man from such a sect who finds himself morally crushed and uprooted, exposed to refined and brutal torture, except to aid the class and his "comrades" with his "confessions"? Such confessions, he is convinced, are necessary to the class to resist the "anti-Socialist" opposition and "imperialists." These confessions are the one "great" and "revolutionary" contribution left that the victim, lost and wrecked, can make.

Every true Communist has been educated and has educated himself and others in the belief that fractions and fractional battles are among the greatest crimes against the party and its aims. It is true that a Communist party which was divided by fractions could neither win in the revolution nor establish its dominance. Unity at any price and without consideration for anything else becomes a mystical obligation behind which the aspirations of the oligarchs for complete power entrench themselves. Even if he has suspected this, or even known it, the demoralized Communist oppositionist has still not freed himself of the mystic idea of unity. Besides, he may think that leaders come and go, and that these too—the evil, the stupid, the egotistical, the inconsequential and the power-loving—will disappear, while the goal will remain. The goal is everything; has it not always been thus in the party?

Trotsky himself, who was the most important of all the oppositionists, did not go much further in his reasoning. In a moment of self-criticism, he shouted that the party is infallible, for it is the incarnation of historical necessity, of a classless society. In attempting to explain, in his exile, the monstrous amorality of the Moscow trials, he leaned on historical analogies: Rome, before the conquest of Christianity; and the Renaissance, at the beginning of capitalism; in both of which also appeared the inevitable phenomena of perfidious murders, calumnies, lies, and monstrous mass crimes. So it must be during the transition to socialism, he concluded; these were the remnants of the old class society which were still evident in the new. However, he did not succeed in explaining anything through this; he only succeeded in appeasing his conscience, in that he did not "betray" the "dictatorship of the proletariat," or the Soviets, as the *one* form of the transition into the new and classless society. If he had gone into the problem more deeply, he would have seen that, in Communism as in the Renaissance and other periods in history, when an ownership class is breaking a trail for itself, moral considerations play a smaller and smaller role as the difficulties of the class increase and as its domination needs to become more complete.

In the same way, those who did not understand what sort of social transformation was actually at stake after the Communists were victorious had to re-evaluate the diverse moral crises among the Communists. The so-called process of de-Stalinization, or the unprincipled, somewhat Stalinist-style, attacks on Stalin by his former courtiers are also re-evaluated as "a moral crisis."

Moral crises, great or small, are inevitable in every dictatorship, for its followers, accustomed to thinking that uniformity of political thought is the greatest patriotic virtue and the most holy civil obligation, must be disturbed over the inevitable reversals and changes.

But the Communists feel and know that their totalitarian domination does not weaken, but rather gets stronger, in such reversals; that this is its inevitable path; and that moral and similar reasons play only a secondary role, if they are not even a hindrance. Practice very rapidly teaches them this. Consequently, their moral crises, no matter how profound, end very quickly. Of course, the Communists cannot be selective in the means they use if they desire to achieve the *real* aim to which they aspire, and which they conceal under the cover of the *ideal* aim.

4.

Moral downgrading in the eyes of other men does not yet mean that Communism is weak. Generally, until now, it has meant the reverse. The various purges and "Moscow trials" strengthened the Communist system and Stalin. In all events, certain strata—the intellectuals with Gide as the most famous example—renounced Communism because of this and doubted that Communism as it is today could realize the ideas and ideals they believed in. However, Communism, such as it is, has not become weaker: the new class has become stronger, more secure, freeing itself from moral considerations, wading in the blood of every adherent of the Communist idea. Although it has been morally downgraded in the eyes of others, Communism has actually been strengthened in the eyes of its own class and in its domination over society.

Other conditions would be necessary for contemporary Communism to be lowered in the estimation of the ranks of its own class. It is necessary for the revolution not only to devour its own children, but—one might say—devour itself. It is necessary for its greatest minds to perceive that it is the exploiting class and that its reign is unjustified. Concretely speaking, it is necessary for the class to perceive that in the near future there cannot be any talk of the withering away of the state, or talk of a Communist society—in which everyone will work according to his capabilities and will receive according to his needs. The class must recognize that the possibility of such a society can as well be refuted as it can be demonstrated. Thus the means that this class used and is using to achieve its aim and dominance would become absurd, inhumane, and contrary to its great purpose—even to the class itself. This would mean that there were cleavages and vacillations, which could not longer be checked, among the ruling class. In other words, the battle for its own existence would drive the ruling class itself, or individual fractions of it, to renounce the current means it is using, or renounce the idea that its goals are within sight and real.

There is no prospect of such a development here as a purely theoretic proposition—in any of the Communist countries, least of all in the post-Stalin U.S.S.R. The ruling class is still a compact one there; the condemnation of Stalin's methods has evolved, even in theory, into protecting the U.S.S.R. from the despotism of a personal dictatorship. At the Twentieth Party Congress, Khrushchev advocated "necessary terrorism" against the "enemy," in contrast to Stalin's despotism against "good Communists." Khrushchev did not condemn Stalin's methods as such, but only their use in the ranks of the ruling class. It seems that the relations within the class, which has become strong enough to avoid surrender to the absolute dominance of its leader and police apparatus, have changed since Stalin. The class itself and its methods have not considerably changed in terms of internal cleavages with regard to moral cohesion. The first signs of cleavage, however, are present; these are evidencing themselves in the ideological crisis. But in spite of this it must be realized that the process of moral disintegration has scarcely begun; the conditions hardly exist for it to happen.

Arrogating certain rights to itself, the ruling oligarchy cannot avoid allowing the crumbs of such rights to fall to the people. It is impossible for the oligarchy to lecture on the lack of rights under Stalin even among the Communists, and not at the same time expect an echo among the masses—who are immeasurably more deprived of their rights. The French bourgeoisie finally rebelled against its emperor, Napoleon, when his wars and bureaucratic despotism became intolerable. But the French people eventually got some profit from this. Stalin's methods, in which the dogmatic hypothesis of a future society also played an important role, will not return. But this does not mean that the current oligarchs will renounce the use of all his means, even though they cannot use them, or that the U.S.S.R. will soon or overnight become a legal, democratic state.

However, something has changed. The ruling class will no longer be able to justify even to itself that the end justifies the means. The class will still lecture on the final goal—a Communist society—for if it did otherwise it would have to renounce absolute dominance. This will force it to resort to any means. Every time that it does resort to them, it will also have to condemn their use. A stronger power—fear of public opinion in the world, fear that it will bring harm to itself and its absolute domination—will sway the class and hold back its hand. Feeling itself sufficiently strong to destroy the cult of its creator, or the creator of the system—Stalin—it simultaneously gave the death blow to its own ideal basis. Completely dominant, the ruling class has begun to abandon and lose the ideology, the dogma which brought it to power. The class has begun to split up into fractions. At the top everything is peaceful and smooth, but below the top, in the depths, and even in its ranks, new thoughts, new ideas, are bubbling and future storms are brewing.

Because it had to renounce Stalin's methods, the ruling class will not be able to preserve its dogma. The methods were actually only the expression of that dogma, and, indeed, of the practice on which the dogma was based.

It was not good will, still less humanity, which prompted Stalin's associates to perceive the harmfulness of Stalin's methods. It was urgent necessity that prompted the ruling class to become more "understanding." But, by avoiding the use of very brutal methods, the oligarchs cannot help but plant the seed of doubt about their goals. The end once served as moral cover for the use of any means. Renouncing the use of such means will arouse doubts as to the end itself. As soon as means which would insure an end are shown to be evil, the end will show itself as being unrealizable. For the essential thing in every policy is first of all the means, assuming that all ends appear good. Even "the road to hell is paved with good intentions."

5.

Throughout history there have been no ideal ends which were attained with non-ideal, inhumane means, just as there has been no free society which was built by slaves. Nothing so well reveals the reality and greatness of ends as the methods used to attain them.

If the end must be used to condone the means, then there is something in the end itself, in its reality, which is not worthy. That which really blesses the end, which justifies the efforts and sacrifices for it, is the means: their constant perfection, humaneness, increasing freedom.

Contemporary Communism has not even reached the beginning of such a situation. Instead, it has stopped dead, hesitating over its means, but always assured about its ends.

No regime in history which was democratic—or relatively democratic while it lasted—was predominantly established on the aspiration for ideal ends, but rather on the small everyday means in sight. Along with this, each such regime achieved, more or less spontaneously, great ends. On the other hand, every despotism tried to justify itself by its ideal aims. Not a single one achieved great ends.

Absolute brutality, or the use of any means, is in accord with the grandiosity, even with the unreality, of Communist aims.

By revolutionary means, contemporary Communism has succeeded in demolishing one form of society and despotically setting up another. At first it was guided by the most beautiful, primordial human ideas of equality and brotherhood; only later did it conceal behind these ideas the establishment of its domination by whatever means.

As Dostoyevski has his hero Shigaliev say, quoted by another character, in *The Possessed:*

> ". . . He's written a good thing in that manuscript," Verkhovensky went on. . . . "Every member of the society spies on the others, and it's his duty to inform against them. Every one belongs to all and all to every one. All are slaves and equal in their slavery. In extreme cases he advocates slander and murder, but the great thing about it is equality. . . . Slaves are bound to be equal. There has never been either freedom or equality without despotism. . . ."

Thus, by justifying the means because of the end, the end itself becomes increasingly more distant and unrealistic, while the frightful reality of the means becomes increasingly obvious and intolerable.

The Essence

1.

None of the theories on the essence of contemporary Com munism treats the matter exhaustively. Neither does this theory claim to do so. Contemporary Communism is the product of a series of historical, economic, political, ideological, national, and international causes. A categorical theory about its essence cannot be entirely accurate.

The essence of contemporary Communism could not even be perceived until, in the course of its development, it revealed itself to its very entrails. This moment came, and could only come, because Communism entered a particular phase of its development—that of its maturity. It then became possible to reveal the nature of its power, ownership, and ideology. In the time that Communism was developing and was predominantly an ideology, it was almost impossible to see through it completely.

Just as other truths are the work of many authors, countries, and movements, so it is with contemporary Communism. Communism has been revealed gradually, more or less parallel to its development; it cannot be looked upon as final, because it has not completed its development.

Most of the theories regarding Communism, however, have

some truth in them. Each of them has usually grasped one aspect of Communism or one aspect of its essence.

There are two basic theses on the essence of contemporary Communism.

The first of them claims that contemporary Communism is a type of new religion. We have already seen that it is neither a religion nor a church, in spite of the fact that it contains elements of both.

The second thesis regards Communism as revolutionary socialism, that is, something which was born of modern industry, or capitalism, and of the proletariat and its needs. We have seen that this thesis also is only partially accurate: contemporary Communism began in well-developed countries as a socialist ideology and a reaction against the suffering of the working masses in the industrial revolution. But after having come into power in underdeveloped areas, it became something entirely different—an exploiting system opposed to most of the interests of the proletariat itself.

The thesis has also been advanced that contemporary Communism is only a contemporary form of despotism, produced by men as soon as they seize power. The nature of the modern economy, which in every case requires centralized administration, has made it possible for this despotism to be absolute. This thesis also has some truth in it: modern Communism is a modern despotism which cannot help but aspire toward totalitarianism. However, all types of modern despotism are not variants of Communism, nor are they totalitarian to the degree that Communism is.

Thus whatever thesis we examine, we find that each thesis explains one aspect of Communism, or a part of the truth, but not the entire truth.

Neither can my theory on the essence of Communism be accepted as complete. This is, anyway, the weakness of every definition, especially when such complex and living matters as social phenomena are being defined.

Nevertheless, it is possible to speak in the most abstract theoretical way about the essence of contemporary Communism, about what is most essential in it, and what permeates all its manifestations and inspires all of its activity. It is possible to penetrate deeper into this essence, to elucidate its various aspects; but the essence itself has already been exposed.

Communism, and likewise its essence, is continuously changing from one form to another. Without this change it cannot even exist. Consequently, these changes require continuous examination and a deeper study of the already obvious truth.

The essence of contemporary Communism is the product of particular conditions, historical and others. But as soon as Communism becomes strong, the essence itself becomes a factor and creates the conditions for its own continued existence. Consequently, it is evident that it is necessary to examine the essence separately according to the form and the conditions in which it appears and is operating at a given moment.

2.

The theory that contemporary Communism is a type of modern totalitarianism is not only the most widespread, but also the most accurate. However, an actual understanding of the term "modern totalitarianism" where Communism is being discussed is not so widespread.

Contemporary Communism is that type of totalitarianism which consists of three basic factors for controlling the people. The first is power; the second, ownership; the third, ideology. They are monopolized by the one and only political party, or—according to my previous explanation and terminology—by a new class; and, at present, by the oligarchy of that party or of that class. No totalitarian system in history, not even a contemporary one—with the exception of Communism—has succeeded in incorporating simultaneously all these factors for controlling the people to this degree.

When one examines and weighs these three factors, power is the one which has played and still continues to play the most important role in the development of Communism. One of the other factors may eventually prevail over power, but it is impossible to determine this on the basis of present conditions. I believe that power will remain the basic characteristic of Communism.

Communism first originated as an ideology, which contained in its seed Communism's totalitarian and monopolistic nature. It can certainly be said that ideas no longer play the main, predominant role in Communism's control of the people. Communism as an ideology has mainly run its course. It does not have many new things to reveal to the world. This could not be said for the other two factors, power and ownership.

It can be said: power, either physical, intellectual, or economic, plays a role in every struggle, even in every social human action. There is some truth in this. It can also be said: in every policy, power, or the struggle to acquire and keep it, is the basic problem and aim. There is some truth in this also. But contemporary Communism is not only such a power; it is something more. It is power of a particular type, a power which unites within itself the control of ideas, authority, and ownership, a power which has become an end in itself.

To date, Soviet Communism, the type which has existed the longest and which is the most developed, has passed through three phases. This is also more or less true of other types of Communism which have succeeded in coming to power (with the exception of the Chinese type, which is still predominantly in the second phase).

The three phases are: revolutionary, dogmatic, and nondogmatic Communism. Roughly speaking, the principal catchwords, aims, and personalities corresponding to these various phases are: Revolution, or the usurpation of power—Lenin. "Socialism," or the building of the system—Stalin. "Legality," or stabilization of the system— "collective leadership."

It is important to note that these phases are not distinctly separate from one another, that elements of all are found in each. Dogmatism abounded, and the "building of socialism" had already begun, in the Leninist period; Stalin did not renounce revolution, or reject the dogmas, which interfered with the building of the system. Present-day, non-dogmatic Communism is only non-dogmatic conditionally: it just will not renounce even the minutest practical advantages for dogmatic reasons. Precisely because of such advantages, it will at the same time be in a position to persecute unscrupulously the minutest doubt concerning the truth or purity of the dogma. Thus, Communism, proceeding from practical needs and capabilities, has today even furled the sails of revolution, or of its own military expansion. But it has not renounced one or the other.

This division into three phases is only accurate if it is taken roughly and abstractly. Clearly separate phases do not actually exist, nor do they correspond to specific periods in the various countries.

The boundaries between the phases, which overlap, and the forms in which the phases appear are varied in different Communist countries. For example, Yugoslavia has passed through all three phases in a relatively short time and with the same personalities at the summit. This is obvious in both precepts and method of operation.

Power plays a major role in all three of these phases. In the revolution it was necessary to seize power; in the building of socialism, it was necessary to create a new system by means of that power; today power must preserve the system.

During the development, from the first to the third phase, the quintessence of Communism—power—evolved from being the means and became an end in itself. Actually power was always more or less the end, but Communist leaders, thinking that through power as a means they would attain the ideal goal, did not believe it to be an end in itself. Precisely because power served as a means for the Utopian transformation of society, it could not avoid becoming an end in itself and the most important aim of Communism. Power was able to appear as a means in the first and second phases. It can no longer be concealed that in the third phase power is the actual principal aim and essence of Communism.

Because of the fact that Communism is being extinguished as an ideology, it must maintain power as the main means of controlling the people.

In revolution, as in every type of war, it was natural to concentrate primarily on power: the war had to be won. During the period of industrialization, concentrating on power could still be considered natural: the construction of industry, or a "socialist society," for which so many sacrifices had been made, was necessary. But as all this is being completed, it becomes apparent that in Communism power has not only been a means but that it has also become the main, if not the sole, end.

Today power is both the means and the goal of Communists, in order that they may maintain their privileges and ownership. But since these are special forms of power and ownership, it is only through power itself that ownership can be exercised. Power is an end in itself and the essence of contemporary Communism. Other classes may be able to maintain ownership without a monopoly over power, or power without a monopoly over ownership. Until now, this has not been possible for the new class, which was formed through Communism; it is very improbable that it will be possible in the future.

Throughout all three of these phases, power has concealed itself as the hidden, invisible, unspoken, natural and principal end. Its role has been stronger or weaker depending on the degree of control over the people required at the time. In the first phase, ideas were the inspiration and the prime mover for the attainment of power; in the second phase, power operated as the whip of society and for its own maintainance; today, "collective ownership" is subordinated to the impulses and needs of power.

Power is the alpha and the omega of contemporary Communism, even when Communism strives to prevent this.

Ideas, philosophical principles and moral considerations, the nation and the people, their history, in part even ownership—all can be changed and sacrificed. But not power. Because this would signify Communism's renunciation of itself, of its own essence. Individuals can do this. But the class, the party, the oligarchy cannot. This is the purpose and the meaning of its existence.

Every type of power besides being a means is at the same time and end—at least for those who aspire to it. Power is almost exclusively an end in Communism, because it is both the source and the guarantee of all privileges. By means of and through power the material privileges and ownership of the ruling class over national goods are realized. Power determines the value of ideas, and suppresses or permits their expression.

It is in this way that power in contemporary Communism differs from all other types of power, and that Communism itself differs from every other system.

Communism has to be totalitarian, exclusive, and isolated precisely because power is the most essential component of Communism. If Communism actually could have had other ends, it would have to make it possible for other forces to spring up in opposition and operate independently.

How contemporary Communism will be defined is secondary. Everyone who undertakes the work of explaining Communism finds himself faced with the problem of defining it, even if actual conditions do not compel him to do this—conditions in which Communists glorify their system as "socialism," "classless society," and "the realization of men's eternal dreams," while the opposing element defines Communism as an insensitive tyranny, the chance success of a terroristic group, and the damnation of the human race.

Science must use already established categories in order to make a simple exposition. Is there any category in sociology into which we can cram contemporary Communism if we use a little force?

In common with many authors who started from other positions, I have, in recent years, equated Communism with state capitalism or, more precisely, with total state capitalism.

This interpretation won out among the leaders of Yugoslav Communists during the time of their clash with the government of the U.S.S.R. But just as Communists, according to practical needs, easily change even their "scientific" analysis, Yugoslav party leaders changed this interpretation after the "reconciliation" with the Soviet government, and once more proclaimed the U.S.S.R. a Socialist country. At the same time, they proclaimed the Soviet imperialistic attack on the independence of Yugoslavia—in Tito's words—a "tragic," "incomprehensible" event, evoked by the "arbitrariness of individuals."

Contemporary Communism for the most part does resemble total state capitalism. Its historical origin and the problems which it had to solve—namely, an industrial transformation similar to the one achieved by capitalism but with the aid of the state mechanism—lead to such a conclusion.

If, under Communism, the state were the owner in the name of society and of the nation, then the forms of political power over society would inevitably change according to the varying needs of society and of the nation. The state by its nature is an organ of unity and harmony in society, and not only a force over it. The state could not be both the owner and ruler in itself. In Communism it is reversed: The state is an instrument and always subordinate exclusively to the interests of one and the same exclusive owner, or of one and the same direction in the economy, and in the other areas of social life.

State ownership in the West might be considered more as

state capitalism than it is in Communist countries. The claim that contemporary Communism is state *capitalism* is prompted by the "pangs of conscience" of those who were disillusioned by the Communist system, but who did not succeed in defining it; they therefore equate its evils with those of capitalism. Since there is really no private ownership in Communism but rather formal state ownership, nothing seems more logical than to attribute all evils to the state. This idea of state capitalism is also accepted by those who see 'less evil" in private capitalism. Therefore they like to point out that Communism is a worse type of capitalism.

To claim that contemporary Communism is a transition to something else leads nowhere and explains nothing. What is not a transition to something else?

Even if it is accepted that it has many of the characteristics of an all-encompassing state capitalism, contemporary Communism also has so many of its own characteristics that it is more precise to consider it a special type of new social system.

Contemporary Communism has its own essence which does not permit it to be confused with any other. Communism, while absorbing into itself all kinds of other elements—feudal, capitalist, and even slave-owning—remains individual and independent at the same time.

National Communism

1.

In essence, Communism is only one thing, but it is realized in different degrees and manners in every country. Therefore it is possible to speak of various Communist systems, i.e., of various forms of the same manifestation.

The differences which exist between Communist states—differences that Stalin attempted futilely to remove by force—are the result, above all, of diverse historical backgrounds. Even the most cursory observation reveals how, for example, contemporary Soviet bureaucracy is not without a connecting link with the Czarist system in which the officials were, as Engels noted, "a distinct class." Somewhat the same thing can also be said of the manner of government in Yugoslavia. When ascending to power, the Communists face in the various countries different cultural and technical levels and varying social relationships, and are faced with different national intellectual characters. These differences develop even farther, in a special way. Because the general causes which brought them to power are identical, and because they have to wage a struggle against common internal and foreign opponents, the Communists in separate countries are immediately compelled to fight jointly and on the basis of a similar ideology. International Communism, which was at one time the task of revolutionaries, eventually transformed itself, as did everything else in Communism, and became the common ground of Communist bureaucracies, fighting one another on nationalistic considerations. Of the former international proletariat, only words and empty dogmas remained. Behind them stood the naked national and international interests, aspirations, and plans of the various Communist oligarchies, comfortably entrenched.

The nature of authority and property, a similar international outlook, and an identical ideology inevitably identify Communist states with one another. Nevertheless, it is wrong to ignore and underestimate the significance of the inevitable diferences in degree and manner betwen Communist states. The degree, manner, and form in which Communism will be realized, or its purpose, is just as much of a given condition for each of them as is the essence of Communism itself. No single form of Communism, no matter how similar it is to other forms, exists in any way other than as national Communism. In order to maintain itself, it must become national.

The form of government and property as well as of ideas differs little or not at all in Communist states. It cannot differ markedly since it has an identical nature—total authority. However, if they wish to win and continue to exist, the Communists must adapt the degree and manner of their authority to national conditions.

The differences between Communist countries will, as a rule, be as great as the extent to which the Communists were independent in coming to power. Concretely speaking, only the Communists of three countries—the Soviet Union, China, and Yugoslavia—independently carried out revolutions or, in their own way and at their own speed, attained power and began "the building of socialism." These three countries remained independent as Communist states even in the period when Yugoslavia was—as China is today—under the most extreme influence of the Soviet Union; that is, in "brotherly love" and in "eternal friendship" with it. In a report at a closed session of the Twentieth Congress, Khrushchev revealed that a clash between Stalin and the Chinese government had barely been averted. The case of the clash with Yugoslavia was not an isolated case, but only the most drastic and the first to occur. In the other Communist countries the Soviet government enforced Communism by "armed missionaries"—its army. The diversity of manner and degree of the development in these countries has still not attained the stage reached in Yugoslavia and China. However, to the extent that ruling bureaucracies gather strength as independent bodies in these countries, and to the extent that they recognize that obedience to and copying of the Soviet Union weaken themselves, they endeavor to "pattern" themselves on Yugoslavia; that is, to develop independently. The Communist East European countries did not become satellites of the U.S.S.R. because they benefited from it, but because they were too weak to prevent it. As soon as they become stronger, or as soon as favorable conditions are created, a yearning for independence and for protection of "their own people" from Soviet hegemony will rise among them.

With the victory of a Communist revolution in a country a new class comes into power and into control. It is unwilling to surrender its own hard-gained *privileges,* even though it subordinates its *interests* to a similar class in another country, solely in the cause of ideological solidarity.

Where a Communist revolution has won victory independently, a separate, distinct path of development is inevitable. Friction with other Communist countries, especially with the Soviet Union as the most important and most imperialistic state, follows. The ruling national bureaucracy in the country where the victorious revolution took place has already become independent in the course of the armed struggle and has tasted the blessings of authority and of "nationalization" of property.

Philosophically speaking, it has also grasped and become conscious of its own essence, "its own state," its authority, on the basis of which it claims equality.

This does not mean that this involves only a clash—when it comes to that—between two bureaucracies. A clash also involves the revolutionary elements of a subordinated country, because they do not usually tolerate domination and they consider that relationships between Communist states must be as ideally perfect as predicted in dogma. The masses of the nation, who spontaneously thirst for independence, cannot remain unperturbed in such a clash. In every case the nation benefits from this: it does not have to pay tribute to a foreign government; and the pressure on the domestic government, which no longer desires, and is not permitted, to copy foreign methods, is also diminished. Such a clash also brings in external forces, other states and movements. However, the nature of the clash and the basic forces in it remain. Neither Soviet nor Yugoslav Communists stopped being what they are—not before, nor during, nor after their mutual bickerings. Indeed, the diverse types of degree and manner with which they insured their monopoly led them mutually to deny the existence of socialism in the opposite camp. After they settled their differences, they again acknowledged the existence of socialism elsewhere, becoming conscious that they must respect mutual differences if they wanted to preserve that which was identical in essence and most important to them.

The subordinate Communist governments in East Europe can, in fact must, declare their independence from the Soviet government. No one can say how far this aspiration for independence will go and what disagreements will result. The result depends on numerous unforeseen internal and external circumstances. However, there is no doubt that a national Communist bureaucracy aspires to more complete authority for itself. This is demonstrated by the anti-Tito processes in Stalin's time in the East European countries; it is shown also by the current unconcealed emphasis on "one's own path to socialism," which has recently come to light sharply in Poland and Hungary. The central Soviet government has found itself in difficulty because of the nationalism existing even in those governments which it installed in the Soviet republics (Ukraine, Caucasia), and still more so with regard to those governments installed in the East European countries. Playing an important role in all of this is the fact that the Soviet Union was unable, and will not be able in the future, to assimilate the economies of the East European countries.

The aspirations toward national independence must of course have greater impetus. These aspirations can be retarded and even made dormant by external pressure or by fear on the part of the Communists of "imperialism" and the "bourgeoisie," but they cannot be removed. On the contrary, their strength will grow.

It is impossible to foresee all of the forms that relations between Communist states will assume. Even if cooperation between Communist states of different countries should in a short time result in mergers and federations, so can clashes between Communist states result in war. An open, armed clash between the U.S.S.R. and Yugoslavia was averted not because of the "socialism" in one or the other country, but because it was not in Stalin's interest to risk a clash of unforeseeable proportions. Whatever will happen between Communist states will depend on all those factors which ordinarily affect political events. The interests of the respective Communist bureaucracies, expressed variously as "national" or as "united," along with the unchecked tendency toward ever increasing independence on a national basis, will, for the time being, play an important role in the relationships among the Communist countries.

2.

The concept of national Communism had no meaning until the end of World War II, when Soviet imperialism was manifested not only with regard to the capitalist but the Communist states as well. This concept developed above all from the Yugoslav-U.S.S.R. clash. The renunciation of Stalin's methods by the "collective leadership" of Khrushchev-Bulganin may perhaps modify relations between the U.S.S.R. and other Communist countries, but it cannot resolve them. In the U.S.S.R. operations are not concerned solely with Communism but are simultaneously concerned with the imperialism of the Great Russian—Soviet—state. This imperialism can change in form and method, but it can no more disappear than can the aspirations of Communists of other countries for independence.

A similar development awaits the other Communist states. According to strength and conditions, they too will attempt to become imperialistic in one way or another.

In the development of the foreign policy of the U.S.S.R. there have been two imperialistic phases. Earlier policy was almost exclusively a matter of expansion by revolutionary propaganda in other countries. At that time there were powerful imperialistic tendencies (as regards the Caucasus) in the policies of its highest leaders. But, in my opinion, there is no satisfactory reason for the revolutionary phase to be categorically considered imperialistic, since at that time it was more defensive than aggressive.

If we do not consider the revolutionary phase as imperialistic, then imperialism began, roughly speaking, with the victory of Stalin, or with the industrialization and establishment of the authority of a new class in the 1930's. This change was clearly shown on the eve of the war when Stalin's government was able to go into action and leave behind pacifist and anti-imperialistic phases. It was even expressed in the change of foreign policy; in place of the jovial and, to a certain extent, principled Litvinov, the unscrupulous and reserved Molotov appeared.

The basic cause of an imperialistic policy is completely hidden in the exploitative and despotic nature of the new class. In order that that class might manifest itself as imperialistic, it was necessary for it to attain a prescribed strength and to appear in appropriate circumstances. It already had this strength when World War II began. The war itself abounded in possiblities for imperialistic combinations. The small Baltic states were not necessary for the security of so large a state as the U.S.S.R., particularly in modern war. These states were non-aggressive and even allies; however, they were an attractive morsel for the insatiable appetite of the Great Russian Communist bureaucracy.

In World War II Communist internationalism, up to that time an integral part of Soviet foreign policy, came into conflict with the interests of the ruling Soviet bureaucracy. With that, the necessity for its organization ceased. The idea of dissolution of the Communist International (Comintern) was conceived, according to Georgi Dimitrov, after the subjugation of the Baltic countries, and in the period of cooperation with Hitler, although it was not effected until the second phase of the war during the period of alliance with the Western states.

The Cominform, consisting of the East European and the French and Italian Communist parties, was created on Stalin's initiative in order to guarantee Soviet domination in the satellite countries and to intensify its influence in western Europe. The Cominform was worse than the former Communist International which, even if it was absolutely dominated by Moscow, at least formally represented all of the parties. The Cominform evolved in the field of real and apparent Soviet influence. The clash with Yugoslavia revealed that it was assigned to subordinate to the Soviet government those Communist states and parties which had begun to weaken because of the internal growth of national Communism. After the death of Stalin the

Cominform was finally dissolved. Even the Soviet government, desiring to avoid major and dangerous quarrels, accepted the so-called separate path to socialism, if not national Communism itself.

These organizational changes had profound economic and political causes. As long as the Communist parties in East Europe were weak and the Soviet Union was not sufficiently strong economically, the Soviet government would have had to resort to administrative methods to subjugate the East European countries, even if there had been no Stalinist arbitrariness and despotism. Soviet imperialism, by political, police and military methods, had to compensate for its own economic and other weaknesses. Imperialism in the military form, which was only an advanced stage of the old Czarist military-feudal imperialism, also corresponded to the internal structure of the Soviet Union in which the police and administrative apparatus, centralized in one personality, played a major role. Stalinism was a mixture of a personal Communist dictatorship and militaristic imperialism.

These forms of imperialism developed: joint stock companies, absorption of the exports of the East European countries by means of political pressure at prices below the world market, artificial formation of a "socialist world market," control of every political act of subordinate parties and states, transformation of the traditional love of Communists toward the "socialist fatherland" into deification of the Soviet state, Stalin, and Soviet practices.

But what happened?

A change within the ruling class was quietly completed in the Soviet Union itself. Similar changes, in another sense, also occurred in the East European countries; new national bureaucracies long for ever increasing consolidation of power and property relations, but at the same time they fall into difficulties because of the hegemonic pressure of the Soviet government. If earlier they had had to renounce national characteristics in order to come to power, now such action had become a hindrance to their further ascendancy to power. In addition, it became impossible for the Soviet government to adhere to the exorbitant and hazardous Stalinist foreign policy of military pressure and isolation and, simultaneously, during the period of the general colonial movements, to hold the European countries in infamous bondage.

The Soviet leaders had to concede, after long vacillation and indecisive argumentation, that the Yugoslav leaders were falsely indicted as Hitlerite and American spies just because they defended the right to consolidate and build a Communist system in their own way. Tito became the most significant personality in contemporary Communism. The principle of national Communism was formally acknowledged. But with that Yugoslavia also ceased to be the exclusive creator of innovations in Communism. The Yugoslav revolution subsided into its groove, and a peaceful and matter-of-fact rule began. With that the love between yesterday's enemies did not become greater, nor were the disagreements terminated. This was merely the beginning of a new phase.

Now the Soviet Union entered into the predominantly economic and political phase of its imperialistic policy. Or so it appears, judging from current facts.

Today national Communism is a general phenomenon in Communism. To varying degrees all Communist movements—except that of the U.S.S.R. against which it is directed—are gripped by national Communism. In its time, in the period of Stalin's ascendancy, Soviet Communism also was national Communism. At that time Russian Communism abandoned internationalism, except as an instrument of its foreign policy. Today Soviet Communism is compelled, even if indefinitely, to acknowledge a new reality in Communism.

Changing internally, Soviet imperialism was also compelled to alter its views toward the external world. From predominantly administrative controls, it advanced toward gradual economic integration with the East European countries. This is being accomplished by means of mutual planning in important branches of economy, in which the local Communist governments today mainly voluntarily concur, still sensing themselves weaker externally and internally.

Such a situation cannot remain for long, because it conceals a fundamental contradiction. On the one hand national forms of Communism become stronger, but on the other, Soviet imperialism does not diminsh. Both the Soviet government and the governments of the East European countries, including Yugoslavia, by means of accords and cooperation, are seeking solutions to mutual problems which influence their very nature —preservation of a given form of authority and of property ownership. However, even if it is possible to effect cooperation with respect to property ownership, it is not possible with respect to authority. Although conditions for further integration with the Soviet Union are being realized, those conditions which lead to the *independence* of the East European Communist governments are being realized even more rapidly. The Soviet Union has not renounced authority in these countries, nor have the governments of these countries renounced their craving to attain something similar to Yugoslav independence. The degree of independence that will be attained will depend on the state of international and internal forces.

Recognition of national forms of Communism, which the Soviet government did with clenched teeth, has immense significance and conceals within itself very considerable dangers for Soviet imperialism.

It involves freedom of discussion to a certain extent; this means ideological independence too. Now the fate of certain heresies in Communism will depend not only on the tolerance of Moscow, but on their national potentialities. Deviation from Moscow that strives to maintain its influence in the Communist world on a "voluntary" and "ideologic" basis cannot possibly be checked.

Moscow itself is no longer that which it was. It single-handedly lost the monopoly of the new ideas and the moral right to prescribe the only permissible "line." Renouncing Stalin, it ceased to be the ideological center. In Moscow itself the epoch of great Communist monarchs and of great ideas came to an end, and the reign of mediocre Communist bureaucrats began.

"Collective leadership" did not anticipate that any difficulties and failures were awaiting it in Communism itself—either externally or internally. But what could it do? Stalin's imperialism was exorbitant and overly dangerous, and what was even worse, ineffective. Under him not only the people generally, but even the Communists, grumbled, and they did so at the time of a very strained international situation.

The world center of Communist ideology no longer exists; it is in the process of complete disintegration. The unity of the world Communist movement is incurably injured. There are no visible possibilities whatsoever that it can be restored. However, just as the shift from Stalin to "collective leadership" did not alter the nature of the system itself in the U.S.S.R., so too national Communism has been unable, despite ever increasing possibilities for liberation from Moscow, to alter its internal nature, which consists of total control and monopoly of ideas, and ownership by the party bureaucracy. Indeed, it significantly alleviated the pressure and slowed down the rate of establishment of its monopoly over property, particularly in the rural areas. But national Communism neither desires nor is able to transform itself into something other than Communism, and something always spontaneously draws it toward its source—toward the Soviet Union. It will be unable to separate its fate from that which links it with the remaining Communist countries and movements.

National modifications in Communism jeopardize Soviet imperialism, particularly the imperialism of the Stalin epoch, but not Communism either as a whole or in essence. On the contrary, where Communism is in control these changes are able to influence its direction and even to strengthen it and make it acceptable externally. National Communism is in harmony with non-dogmaticism, that is, with the anti-Stalinist phase in the development of Communism. In fact, it is a basic form of this phase.

3.

National Communism is unable to alter the nature of current international relationships between states or within workers' movements. But its role in these relationships may be of great significance.

Thus, for example, Yugoslav Communism, as a form of national Communism, played an extremely important role in the weakening of Soviet imperialism and in the downgrading of Stalinism inside the Communist movement. The motives for changes which are occurring in the Soviet Union and in the East European countries are to be found, above all, in the countries themselves. They appeared first in Yugoslavia—in the Yugoslav way. And there, too, they were first completed. Thus Yugoslav Communism as national Communism, in the clash with Stalin, actually originated a new, post-Stalin phase in the development of Communism. Yugoslav Communism significantly influenced changes in Communism itself, but did not fundamentally influence either international relationships or non-Communist workers' movements.

The expectation that Yugoslav Communism would be able to evolve toward democratic socialism or that it would be able to serve as a bridge between Social Democracy and Communism has proved baseless. The Yugoslav leaders themselves were in conflict over this question. During the time of Soviet pressure on Yugoslavia they demonstrated a fervent desire for a *rapprochement* with the Social Democrats. However, in 1956, during the period of peace with Moscow, Tito announced that both the Cominform and the Socialist International were unnecessary, despite the fact that the Socialist International unselfishly defended Yugoslavia while the Cominform laboriously attacked Yugoslavia. Preoccupied with a policy of so-called active coexistence, which for the most part corresponds to their interests of the moment, the Yugoslav leaders declared that both organizations—the Cominform and the Socialist International—were "immoderate" solely because they were allegedly the product of two blocs.

The Yugoslav leaders confused their desires with reality and confused their momentary interests with profoundly historic and socialistic differences.

At any rate, the Cominform was the product of Stalinist efforts for the creation of an Eastern military bloc. It is impossible to deny the fact that the Socialist International is linked with the Western bloc, or with the Atlantic Pact, since it operates within the framework of the West European countries. But it would exist even without that bloc. It is, above all, an organization of Socialists of the developed European countries in which political democracy and similar relationships exist.

Military alliances and blocs are temporary manifestations, but the Western Socialism and Eastern Communism reflect much more enduring and basic tendencies.

Contrasts between Communism and a Social Democracy are not the result of different principles only—these least of all—but of the opposing directions of economic and intellectual forces. The clash between Martov and Lenin at the Second Congress of Russian Social Democrats in London in 1903 concerning the question of party membership, and concerning the question of lesser or greater centralism and discipline in the party—which Deutscher correctly calls the beginning of the greatest schism in history—was of far greater significance than even its initiators were able to anticipate. With that began not only the formation of two movements but of two social systems.

The schism between Communists and Social Democrats is

impossible to bridge until the very natures of these movements, or the conditions themselves which resulted in differences between them, are changed. In the course of a half century, despite periodic and separate *rapprochements,* the differences have on the whole increased, and their natures have become still more individualized. Today Social Democracy and Communism are not only two movements but two worlds.

National Communism, separating itself from Moscow, has been unable to bridge this chasm although it can circumvent it. This was demonstrated by the cooperation of the Yugoslav Communists with the Social Democrats, which was more seeming than actual and more courteous than sincere, and which was without tangible important results for either side.

For completely different reasons, unity has not even been realized between Western and Asian Social Democrats. The differences between them were not as great in essence, or in principle, as they were in practice. For national reasons of their own, Asian Socialists had to remain separated from West European Socialists. Even when they are opponents of colonialism, Western Socialists—though they play no leading role—are representatives of countries which, solely because they are more developed, exploit the undeveloped countries. The contrast between Asian and Western Social Democrats is a manifestation of contrasts between underdeveloped and developed countries, carried over into the ranks of the Socialist movement. Despite the fact that concrete forms of this contrast have to be sharply defined, proximity in essence—as far as can be deduced today—is obvious and inevitable.

4.

National Communism similar to that in Yugoslavia could be of immense international significance in Communist parties of non-Communist states. It could be of even greater significance there than in Communist parties which are actually in power. This is relevant above all to the Communist parties in France and Italy, which encompass a significant majority of the working class and which are, along with several parties in Asia, the only ones of major significance in the non-Communist world.

Until now, the manifestations of national Communism in these parties have been without major significance and impetus. However, they have been inevitable. They could, in the final analysis, lead to profound and essential changes in these parties.

These parties have to contend with the Social Democrats—who are able to channel the dissatisfied masses toward themselves by means of their own socialist slogans and activity. This is not the only reason for the eventual deviation of these parties from Moscow. Lesser reasons may be seen in the periodic and unanticipated reversals of Moscow and of the other ruling Communist parties. Such reversals lead these and other non-ruling Communist parties into a "crisis of conscience"—to spit on what until yesterday they extolled, then suddenly to change their line. Neither oppositionist propaganda nor administrative pressure will play a fundamental role in the transformation of these parties.

The basic causes for deviation of these parties from Moscow may be found in the nature of the social system of the countries in which they operate. If it becomes evident—and it appears likely—that the working class of these countries is able through parliamentary forms to arrive at some improvement in its position, and also to change the social system itself, the working class will abandon the Communists regardless of its revolutionary and other traditions. Only small groups of Communist dogmaticists can look dispassionately at the disassociation of the workers; serious political leaders in a given nation will endeavor to avoid it even at the cost of weakening ties with Moscow.

Parliamentary elections which give a huge number of votes

to Communists in these countries do not accurately express the actual strength of Communist parties. To a significant degree they are an expression of dissatisfaction and delusion. Stubbornly following the Communist leaders, the masses will just as easily abandon them the moment it becomes obvious to them that the leaders are sacrificing national institutions, or the concrete prospects of the working class, to their bureaucratic nature, or to the "dictatorship of the proletariat" and ties with Moscow.

Of course, all of this is hypothesis. But even today these parties are finding themselvs in a difficult situation. If they really wish to be adherents of parliamentarianism, their leaders will have to renounce their anti-parliamentary nature, or change over to their own national Communism which would, since they are not in control, lead to disintegration of their parties.

The leaders of Communist parties in these countries are driven to experiment with the idea of national Communism and national forms by all of these factors: by the strengthening of the possibility that the transformation of society and the improvement of position of the workers will be attained by democratic means; by Moscow's reversals, which by the downgrading of the cult of Stalin ultimately resulted in destruction of the ideologic center; by concurrence of the Social Democrats; by tendencies toward unification of the West on a profound and enduring social basis as well as a military one; by military strengthening of the Western bloc which offers increasingly fewer prospects for "brotherly aid" for the Soviet army; and by the impossibility of new Communist revolutions without a world war. At the same time fear of the inevitable result of a transition to parliamentarianism, and of a breaking off with Moscow, prevents these leaders from doing anything of real significance. Increasingly deeper social differences between the East and the West work with relentless force. The clever

Togliatti is confused, and the robust Thorez is wavering. External and internal party life is beginning to bypass them.

Emphasizing that today a parliament can serve as a "form of transition to socialism," Khrushchev intended at the Twentieth Congress to facilitate manipulation of the Communist parties in "capitalist countries," and to stimulate the cooperation of Communists and Social Democrats and the formation of "People's Fronts." Something like this appeared realistic to him, according to his words, because of the changes which had resulted in the strengthening of Communism and because of peace in the world. With that he tacitly acknowledged to everyone the obvious impossibility of Communist revolutions in the developed countries, as well as the impossibility of further expansion of Communism under current conditions without the danger of a new world war. The policy of the Soviet state has been reduced to a status quo, while Communism has descended to gradual acquisition of new positions in a new way.

A crisis has actually begun in the Communist parties of the non-Communist states. If they change over to national Communism, they risk forsaking their very nature; and if they do not change over, they face a loss of followers. Their leaders, those who represent the spirit of Communism in these parties, will be forced into the most cunning manipulations and unscrupulous measures if they are to extricate themselves from this contradiction. It is improbable that they will be able to check disorientation and disintegration. They have reached a state of conflict with the real tendencies of development in the world and in their countries that obviously lead toward new relationships.

National Communism outside of the Communist states inevitably leads toward renunciation of Communism itself, or toward the disintegration of the Communist parties. Its possibilities are greater today in the non-Communist states, but obviously, only along the lines of separation from Communism itself. Therefore, national Communism in these parties will emerge victorious only with difficulty and slowly, in successive outbursts.

In the Communist parties that are not in power it is evident that national Communism—despite its intent to stimulate Communism and strengthen its nature—is simultaneously the heresy that nibbles at Communism as such. National Communism per se is contradictory. Its nature is the same as that of Soviet Communism, but it aspires to detach itself into something of its own, nationally. In reality, national Communism is Communism in decline.

The Present-Day World

1.

In order to determine more clearly the international position of contemporary Communism, it is necessary briefly to draw a picture of the present-day world.

The results of the First World War led to the transformation of Czarist Russia into a new type of state, or into a country with new types of social relationships. Internationally the difference between the technical level and tempo of the United States and the countries of western Europe deepened; the Second World War was to transform this into an unbridgeable gulf, so that only the United States did not undergo major changes in the structure of its economy.

Wars were not the only cause of this gulf between the United States and the rest of the world; they only accelerated its coming. The reasons for the rapid advancement of the United States can be found, undoubtedly, in its internal potentialities—in the natural and social conditions and the character of the economy. American capitalism developed in different circumstances from European capitalism and it was in full swing at a time when its European counterpart had already begun to decline.

Today the gulf is this wide: 6 per cent of the world population, that of the United States, produces 40 per cent of the goods and services in the world. Between the First and Second World Wars the United States contributed 33 per cent of world production; after the Second World War it contributed 50 per cent. The opposite was true of Europe (excluding the U.S.S.R.), whose contribution to world production dropped from 68 per cent in 1870, to 42 per cent in the 1925-29 period, then to 34 per cent in 1937, and to 25 per cent in 1948 (according to United Nations data).

The development of modern industry in colonial economies was also of special importance, and it was to make it possible for most of them, ultimately, to gain their freedom after the Second World War.

In the period between the First and Second World Wars capitalism went through an economic crisis so profound and with consequences so great that only dogma-ridden Communist brains, particularly those in the U.S.S.R., failed to acknowledge it. In contrast to the crises of the nineteenth century, the great crisis of 1929 revealed that such cataclysms today signify danger to the social order itself, even to the life of the nation as a whole. The developed countries—first of all the United States—had to find ways to emerge from this crisis gradually. By various methods the United States resorted to a planned economy on a national scale. The changes in connection with this were of epochal importance for the developed countries and for the rest of the world, although they were not recognized sufficiently from a theoretical point of view.

In this period various forms of totalitarianism developed in the U.S.S.R. and in capitalist countries such as Nazi Germany.

Germany, in contrast to the United States, was not capable of solving the problem of its internal and external expansion by normal economic means. War and totalitarianism (Nazism) were the only outlets for the German monopolists, and they subordinated themselves to the racist war party.

As we have seen, the U.S.S.R. went over to totalitarianism

for other reasons. It was the condition for its industrial transformation.

However, there was another, perhaps not very obvious, element which was really revolutionary for the modern world. This element was modern wars. They lead to substantial changes even when they do not lead to actual revolutions. Leaving frightful devastation behind them, they change both world relations and relations within individual countries.

The revolutionary character of modern wars is manifested not only in the fact that they give impetus to technical discoveries, but, most of all, in the fact that they change the economic and social structure. In Great Britain, the Second World War exposed and affected relationships to the extent that considerable nationalization became inevitable. India, Burma, and Indonesia emerged from the war as independent countries. The unification of western Europe began as a result of the war. It hurled the United States and the U.S.S.R. to the summit as the two major economic and political powers.

Modern warfare affects the life of nations and humanity much more deeply than did wars of earlier epochs. There are two reasons for this: First, modern war must inevitably be total war. Not one economic, human, or other source can remain untapped, because the technical level of production is already so high that it makes it impossible for parts of any nation or any branch of the economy to stand to one side. Second, for the same technical, economic, and other reasons, the world, to an incomparably larger extent, has become a whole; so the smallest changes in one part bring forth reactions in other parts as well. Every modern war tends to change into a world war.

These invisible military and economic revolutions are of enormous extent and significance. They are more spontaneous than revolutions achieved by force; that is, they are not burdened to as great an extent with ideological and organizational elements. Therefore, such revolutions make it possible to register in a more orderly way the tendencies of movements in the modern world.

The world as it is today and as it emerged from the Second World War is obviously not the same as it was before.

Atomic energy, which man has torn out of the heart of matter and wrested from the cosmos, is the most spectacular but not the only sign of a new epoch.

Official Communist prognostications on the future of the human race declare that atomic energy is the symbol of Communist society, just as steam was the symbol and the power prerequisite of industrial capitalism. However we interpret this naïve and biased reasoning, another point is true: atomic energy is already leading to changes in individual countries and in the world as a whole. Certainly these changes do not point toward that Communism and socialism which the Communist "theoreticians" desire.

Atomic energy, as a discovery, is not the fruit of one nation, but of a century of work by hundreds of the most brilliant minds of many nations. Its application is also the result of the efforts—not only scientific but economic—of a number of countries. If the world had not already been unified, neither the discovery nor the application of atomic energy would have been possible.

The effect of atomic energy, in the first place, will tend toward the further unification of the world. On the way, it will shatter inexorably all inherited obstacles—ownership relations and social relations, but above all exclusive and isolated systems and ideologies, such as Communism both before and after Stalin's death.

2.

The tendency toward the unification of the world is the basic characteristic of our time. This does not mean that the world did not earlier have a tendency toward unity, in a different way. The tendency toward binding the world together by means of the world market was already dominant in the mid-nineteenth century. It, too, was an epoch of capitalist economies and national wars. World unity of one kind was being achieved then, through national economies and national wars.

The further unification of the world was effected by the shattering of pre-capitalist forms of production in the undeveloped regions and their division among the developed countries and their monopolies. This was the period of monopolistic capitalism, colonial conquests, and wars in which internal connections and interests of the monopolies often played a role more decisive than national defense itself. The tendencies at that time toward world unity were achieved mainly through conflicts and associations of monopolistic capital. This was a higher level of unity than unity of the market. Capital poured out of national sources, penetrated, took hold, and dominated the entire world.

The present tendencies toward unity are apparent in other areas. They may be found in a very high level of production, in contemporary science, and in scientific and other thought. Further advancement of unity is no longer possible on exclusively national foundations or through the division of the world into individual, monopolistic spheres of influence.

The trends toward this new unity—unity of production—are being built on the foundations already attained in earlier stages—that is, on the unity of the market and the unity of capital. They conflict, however, with already strained and inadequate national, governmental, and, above all, social relations. While the former unities were achieved by means of national struggles or through conflicts and wars over spheres of interest, contemporary unity is being formed, and can only be formed, by the destruction of the social relationships of previous periods.

No one can say conclusively in what manner the coordination and unification of world production will be effected, whether by war or by peaceful means. But there can be no doubt that its tendency cannot be checked.

The first method of unification—war—would hasten unification by force, that is, by the domination of one or another group. But it would inevitably leave behind it the sparks of new conflagrations, discord, and injustice. Unification by means of war would take place at the expense of the weak and defeated. Even if war should bring order into given relationships it would leave behind it unresolved conflicts and deeper misunderstandings.

Because the present world conflict is unfolding mainly on the basis of opposition between systems, it has more of the character of a class conflict than of opposition between nations and states. That is the reason for its unusual severity and sharpness. Any future war would be more of a world and civil war between governments and nations. Not only would the course of the war itself be frightful; its effects on further free development would be terrible too.

The unification of the world by peaceful means, although a slower way, is the only steady, wholesome, and just way.

It appears that the unification of the contemporary world will be effected through the opposition of systems, in contrast to the types of opposition (national) through which unification was achieved in earlier periods.

This does not mean that all contemporary conflicts are merely due to conflicts between systems. There are other conflicts, including those from former epochs. Through the conflict of systems the tendency toward world unity of production is revealing itself most clearly and actively.

It would be unrealistic to expect the unity of world production to be achieved in the near future. The process will take a long time, since it will be the fruit of the organized efforts of the economic and other leading powers of humanity, and because complete unity of production actually cannot be achieved.

The earlier unities were never attained as something final; this unity too is being established only as a tendency, as something toward which production, at least that of the most developed countries, aspires.

3.

The ending of the Second World War had already confirmed the tendency to division of systems on a world scale. All the countries which fell under Soviet influence, even parts of countries (Germany, Korea), achieved more or less the same system. It was the same on the Western side.

The Soviet leaders were fully aware of this process. I remember that at an intimate party in 1945 Stalin said: "In modern war, the victor will impose his system, which was not the case in past wars." He said this before the war was over, at a time when love, hope, and trust were at their peak among the Allies. In February 1948 he said to us, the Yugoslavs, and to the Bulgarians: "They, the Western powers, will make a country of their own out of West Germany and we will make one of our own out of East Germany—this is inevitable."

Today it is fashionable, and to some extent justifiable, to evaluate Soviet policy as it was before and after Stalin's death. However, Stalin did not invent the systems, nor do those who succeeded him believe in them less than he did. What has changed since his death is the method by which Soviet leaders handle relations between systems, not the systems themselves. Did not Khrushchev, at the Twentieth Party Congress, mention his "world of socialism," his "world socialist system," as something separate and special? In practice this means nothing more than insistence upon a division into systems, into the further exclusiveness of Communism's own system and hegemonistic control.

Because the conflict between the West and East is essentially a conflict of systems, it must take on the appearance of an ideological struggle. Ideological war does not wane, even when temporary compromises are effected, and it drugs into unconsciousness the minds in the opposing camps. The more the conflict in the material, economic, political, and other spheres sharpens, the more it seems as if pure ideas themselves were in conflict.

In addition to the exponents of Communism and capitalism there is a third type of country, that which has wrested itself from colonial dependence (India, Indonesia, Burma, the Arab countries, etc.). These countries are straining to construct independent economies in order to tear themselves loose from economic dependence. In them overlap several epochs and a number of systems, and particularly the two contemporary systems.

These emerging nations are, principally for their own national reasons, the most sincere supporters of the slogans of national sovereignty, peace, mutual understanding, and similar ideas. However, they cannot eliminate the conflict between the two systems. They can only alleviate it. In addition they are the very fields of battle between the two systems. Their role can be a significant and noble one but, for the present, not a decisive one.

It is important to observe that both systems claim that the unification of the world will be modeled on one or the other. Both take the stand, then, that there is a need for world unity. However, these stands are diametrically opposed. The modern world's tendency toward unity is being demonstrated and realized through a struggle between opposing forces, a struggle of unheard-of severity in times of peace.

The ideological and political expressions of this struggle are, as we know, Western democracy and Eastern Communism.

Since the unorganized tendencies toward unification are bursting forth more strongly in the West, because of political democracy and a higher technical and cultural level, the West also appears as the champion of political and intellectual freedom.

One or another characteristic system of ownership in these countries may check or stimulate this tendency, depending upon circumstances. However, the aspiration toward unity is widespread. A definite obstacle to this unification is the monopolies. They want unity, in their own interests, but they want to accomplish it by an already obsolete method—in the form of spheres of influence. However, their opponents—for example, the English Labourites—are also adherents of unity, but in a different way. The tendency toward unity is also strong in Great Britain, which has carried out nationalization. Moreover, the United States is carrying out nationalization as well, on an even vaster scale, not by changing the form of ownership, but by putting a considerable portion of the national income into the hands of the government. If the United States should achieve a completely nationalized economy, tendencies toward the unification of the contemporary world would receive still greater impetus.

4.

The law of society and man is to expand and perfect production. This law evidences itself in the contemporary level of science, technology, thought, etc., as a tendency toward the unification of world production. This is a tendency which, as a rule, is so much more irresistible if it involves people on a higher cultural and material level.

Western tendencies toward world unification are the expression of economic, technical, and other needs and, behind these, of political ownership and other forces. The picture in the Soviet camp is different. Even if there had not been other reasons, the Communist East, because it was more backward, would have been compelled to isolate itself economically and ideologically and to compensate for its economic and other weaknesses by political measures.

It may sound strange, but this is true: Communism's so-called socialist ownership is the main obstacle to world unification. The collective and total dominance of the new class creates an isolated political and economic system which impedes the unification of the world. This system can and does change, but very slowly, and almost not at all in regard to mixing and interweaving with other systems in the direction of consolidation. Its changes are made solely for the purpose of increasing its own strength. Leading to one type of ownership, government, and ideas, this system inevitably isolates itself. It inevitably moves toward exclusiveness.

A united world which even the Soviet leaders desire can only be imagined by them as more or less identical with their own and as being theirs. The peaceful coexistence of systems of which they speak does not mean to them the interweaving of various systems, but the static continuation of one system alongside another, until the point when the other system—the capitalist system—is either defeated or corrodes from within.

The existence of the conflict between the two systems does not mean that national and colonial conflicts have ceased. On the contrary, it is through clashes of a national and colonial nature that the basic conflict of systems is revealed. The struggle over the Suez Canal could hardly be kept from turning into strife betwen the two systems, instead of remaining what it was: a dispute between Egyptian nationalism and world trade which, by a coincidence, happened to be represented by the old colonial powers of Britain and France.

Extreme strain in all aspects of international life has been the inevitable result of such relations. Cold war has become the normal peacetime state of the modern world. Its forms have changed and are changing; it becomes milder or more severe, but it is no longer possible to eliminate it under given conditions. It is necessary first to eliminate something much deeper, something which is in the nature of the contemporary world, of contemporary systems, and especially of Communism. The cold war, today the cause of increasing tension, was itself the product of other, deeper, and earlier conflicting factors.

The world in which we live is a world of uncertainty. It is a world of stupefying and unfathomable horizons which science is revealing to humanity; it is also a world of terrible fear of cosmic catastrophe, threatened by modern means of war.

This world will be changed, in one way or another. It cannot remain as it is, divided and with an irresistible aspiration toward unity. World relationships which finally emerge from this entanglement will be neither ideal nor without friction. However, they will be better than the present-day ones.

The present conflict of systems, however, does not indicate that humanity is going in the direction of a single system. This type of conflict demonstrates only that the further unification of the world or, more accurately expressed, the unification of world production, will be achieved through the conflict between systems.

The tendency toward unity of world production cannot lead everywhere to the same type of production, that is, to the same forms of ownership, government, etc. This unity of production expresses the aspiration toward elimination of inherited and artificial obstacles to the flourishing and greater efficiency of modern production. It means a fuller adjustment of production to local, natural, national, and other conditions. The tendency toward this unification really leads to a greater coordination and use of the world production potential.

It is fortunate that a single system does not prevail in the world. On the contrary, the unfortunate thing is that there are too few different systems. Most of all, what is really bad is the exclusive and isolated nature of systems, of whatever kind they may be.

Increasingly greater differences between social units, state and political systems, in addition to increasingly greater efficiency of production, is one of the laws of society. Peoples unite, man conforms more and more to the world around him, but at the same time he also becomes more and more individualized.

The future world will probably be more varied, and, as such, more unified. Its imminent unification will be made possible by variety, not by sameness of type and personality. At least that is the way it has been up to this time. Sameness of type and personality would mean slavery and stagnation; not a higher degree of freedom for production than today's.

A nation which does not become aware of actual world processes and tendencies will have to pay for it dearly. It will inevitably lag behind and in the end will have to adjust to the unification of the world, no matter what its numerical and military strength may be. None will escape this, just as in the past not one nation could resist the penetration of capital and the connection with other nations through the world market.

That is also the reason why today every autarchical, or exclusive, national economy—whatever its form of ownership or political order, or even its technical level—must fall into unresolvable contradictions and stagnation. This holds true also for social systems, ideas, etc. The isolated system can offer only a very modest living; it would be unable to move forward and solve the problems brought about by modern techniques and modern ideas.

Incidentally, world development has already demolished the Communist-Stalinist theory of the possibility of construction of a socialist, or Communist, society in one country, and has brought about the strengthening of the totalitarian despotism, or the absolute dominance of a new exploiting class.

In these circumstances the construction of a socialist, or Communist, or any other kind of society in one country, or in a large number of countries cut off from the world as a whole, inevitably results in autarchy and the consolidation of despotism. It also causes the weakening of the national potentialities for economic and social progress of the countries concerned. It is possible to have, in harmony with progressive economic and democratic aspirations in the world, more bread and liberty for people generally, a more just distribution of goods, and a normal tempo of economic development. The condition for this is the changing of existing property and political relationships, particularly those in Communism since they are, because of the monopoly of the ruling class, the most serious—although not the only—obstacle to national and world progress.

5.

The tendency toward unification, for other reasons, has also influenced changes in property relationships.

The increased, and even decisive, role of government organs in the economy, and to a large extent in ownership as well, is also an expression of the tendency toward world unification. Certainly it is manifested in different ways in various systems and countries, and even as an obstacle in those places where—as in the Communist countries—formal state ownership itself conceals the monopoly and the total domination of a new class.

In Great Britain private or, more accurately expressed, monopolist ownership has already legally lost its sanctity and purity through Labourite nationalization. Over twenty per cent of British productive power has been nationalized. In the Scandinavian countries, in addition to state ownership, a cooperative type of collective ownership is developing.

The increasing role of government in the economy is especially characteristic of the countries which until recently were colonies and semi-dependent countries, without regard to whether they have a socialist government (Burma), a parliamentary democracy (India), or a military dictatorship (Egypt).

The government makes most of the investments; it controls exports, seizes a large portion of the export funds, etc. The government appears everywhere as an initiator of economic change, and nationalization is a more frequently occurring form of ownership.

The situation is no different in the United States, the country where capitalism is most highly developed. Not only can everybody see the increasing role of the government in the economy from the great crisis (1929) to the present time, but few people deny the inevitability of this role.

James Blaine Walker emphasizes, in *The Epic of American Industry:** "The growing intimacy between government and the economic life has been one of the striking characteristics of the twentieth century."

Walker cites that in 1938 about 20 per cent of the national income was socialized, while in 1940 this percentage went up to at least 25 per cent. Systematic government planning of the national economy began with Roosevelt. At the same time, the number of government workers and government functions, particularly those of the federal government, is growing.

Johnson and Kross, in *The Origins and Development of the American Economy,*† come to the same conclusions. They affirm that administration has been separated from ownership and that the role of the government as a creditor has grown considerably. "One of the chief characteristics of the 20th century," they say, "is the constant augmentation of the government's, especially the federal government's, influence over economic affairs."

In his work *The American Way,*‡ Shepard B. Clough cites figures that illustrate these statements. The expenditures and public debts of the federal government, according to him, look like this:

* New York, Harper, 1949.
† New York, Prentice-Hall, 1953.
‡ New York, T. Y. Crowell, 1953.

Year	*Expenditures of the Federal Government (in millions of dollars)*	*Public Debts (Federal) (in thousands of dollars)*
1870	309.6	2,436,453
1940	8,998.1	42,967,531
1950	40,166.8	256,708,000

In this work Clough speaks of the "managerial revolution," which he understands to be the rise of professional administrators, without whom owners can no longer operate. Their number, role, and solidarity are continually growing in the United States, and men of great business genius, like John D. Rockefeller, John Wanamaker, Charles Schwab and others, do not emerge any longer in the United States.

Fainsod and Gordon, in *Government and the American Economy,** remark that the government has already played a role in the economy and that various social groups have tried to make use of this role in economic life. However, there are now essential differences in this. The regulative role of government, they write, has appeared not only in the sphere of labor but in production—in branches of the economy as important to the nation as transportation, natural gas, coal, and petroleum. "Novel and far-reaching changes were also evident in the form of an expansion of public enterprise and increased concern with the conservation of natural and human resources. Public enterprise became particularly important in the banking and credit field, in electricity, and in the provision of low-cost housing." They comment that the government has begun to play a far more important role than it played half a century ago, even ten years ago. "The result of these developments has been to produce a 'mixed economy,' an economy in which public enterprise, partially government-controlled private en-

* New York, W. W. Norton, 1941.

terprise, and relatively uncontrolled private enterprise all exist side by side."

These and other authors cite various aspects of this process and the growth of the needs of society for social welfare, education, and similar benefits, which are being provided by government agencies, as well as the continual increase—both relative and absolute—in the number of persons employed by the government.

It is understandable that this process received immense impetus and intensity during the Second World War because of military needs. However, after the war the process did not subside but continued at a faster tempo than during the prewar period. It was not just the fact that the Democratic Party was in power. Even the Republican government of Eisenhower, which was elected to power in 1952 on the slogan of a return to private initiative, could not change anything essentially. The same thing happened with the Conservative government in Great Britain; it did not succeed in bringing about denationalization except in the steel industry. Its role in the economy, by comparison with that of the Labour government, has not essentially decreased, although it has not increased either.

The interference of the government in the economy is obviously the result of objective tendencies which had already penetrated the people's consciousness a long time ago. All serious economists, beginning with Keynes, have advocated the intervention of the state in the economy. Now this is more or less an actuality throughout the world. State intervention and state ownership are today an essential and in some places a determining factor in the economy.

One could almost conclude from this that there is no distinction or source of conflict in the fact that in the Eastern system the state plays the major role, while in the Western system private ownership, or ownership by monopolies and companies, plays a major role. Such a conclusion seems all the more warranted since the role of private ownership in the West is gradually declining, the role of the state growing.

However, this is not the case. Aside from the other differences between systems, there is an essential difference in state ownership and in the role of the state in the economy. Though state ownership is technically present to some extent in both systems, they are two different, even contradictory types of ownership. This applies to the role of the state in the economy, too.

Not a single Western government acts like an owner with relation to the economy. In fact, a Western government is neither the owner of nationalized property nor the owner of funds which it has collected through taxes. It cannot be an owner because it is subject to change. It must administer and distribute this property under the control of a parliament. In the course of distribution of property, the government is subject to various influences, but it is not the owner. All it does is administer and distribute, well or badly, property which does not belong to it.

This is not the case in Communist countries. The government both administers and distributes national property. The new class, or its executive organ—the party oligarchy—both acts as the owner and is the owner. The most reactionary and bourgeois government can hardly dream of such a monopoly in the economy.

Surface similarities in ownership in the West and the East are in fact real and deep differences, even conflicting elements.

6.

Even after the First World War, forms of ownership were probably an essential reason for the conflicts between the West and the U.S.S.R. Monopolies then played a much more important role and they could not accept the idea that one part of the world—specifically the U.S.S.R.—was escaping from their domain. The Communist bureaucracy had just recently become the ruling class.

Ownership relationships have always been vital to the U.S.S.R. in its dealings with other countries. Wherever possible its peculiar type of ownership and political relationship was imposed by force. No matter how much it developed its business connections with the rest of the world, it could not go beyond the mere exchange of goods, which had been developed during the period of national states. This was also true of Yugoslavia in the period of its break with Moscow. Yugoslavia could not develop any kind of significant economic cooperation except for the exchange of goods, although she had and continues to have hopes of achieving this. Her economy has remained isolated too.

There are other elements which complicate this picture and these relationships. If the strengthening of Western tendencies toward world unity of production might not mean aid to undeveloped countries, in practice it would lead to the ascendancy of one nation—the United States—or, at best, a group of nations.

By the very element of exchange, the economy and the national life of the undeveloped countries are exploited and forced to be subordinated to the developed countries. This means that the undeveloped countries can only defend themselves by political means, and by shutting themselves in if they wish to survive. This is one way. The other way is to receive aid from the outside, from the developed countries. There is no third way. Up to now there has been barely the beginning along the second way—aid in insignificant amounts.

Today the difference between the American and the Indonesian worker is greater than that between the American worker and the wealthy American stockholder. In 1949 every inhabitant of the United States earned an average of at least $1,440.00; the Indonesian worker earned 1/53rd as much, only $27.00, according to United Nations data. And there is general agreement that the material and other differences between developed and undeveloped countries do not diminish; on the contrary, they increase.

The inequality between the Western developed countries and the undeveloped countries reveals itself as being mainly economic. Traditional political domination by governors and local lords is already on its way out. Now, as a rule, the economy of an undeveloped but politically independent, national government is subordinate to some other country.

Today no single people can willingly accept such subordinate relationships, just as no single people can willingly renounce the advantages made possible by greater productivity.

To ask American or West European workers—not to mention owners—willingly to renounce the benefits offered them by a high level of technology and more productive work is as unthinkable as it would be to persuade a poor Asiatic that he should be happy that he receives so little for his work.

Mutual aid between governments and the gradual elimination of economic and other inequalities between peoples must be born of need in order to become the child of good will.

In the main, economic aid has thus far been extended only in those cases where undeveloped countries, with low purchasing power and low production, have become a burden to the developed countries. The current conflict between the two systems is the main obstacle to the extension of real economic aid. This is not only because huge sums are being spent for military and similar needs; contemporary relationships also hinder the flourishing of production, and its tendency toward unification, thus blocking aid to underdeveloped countries and the progress of the developed countries themselves.

Material and other differences between the developed and the undeveloped countries have also been registered in their internal life. It would be completely inaccurate to interpret democracy in the West only as an expression of solidarity of rich nations in looting the poor ones; the Western countries were democratic long before the time of colonial extra-profits, though on a lower level than that of today. The only connection between present-day democracy in the Western countries and that of the period when Marx and Lenin were alive lies in the fact of continuous development between the two periods. The similarity between past and present democracy is not greater than that between liberal or monopolistic capitalism and modern statism.

In his work, *In Place of Fear,* the British socialist Aneurin Bevan observed:

> It is necessary to distinguish between the intention of Liberalism and its achievements. Its intention was to win power for the new forms of property thrown up by the Industrial Revolution. Its achievement was to win political power for the people irrespective of property.*
>
> . . The function of parliamentary democracy, under universal franchise, historically considered, is to expose wealth-privilege to the attack of the people. It is a sword pointed at the heart of property-power. The arena where the issues are joined is Parliament.†

Bevan's observation applies to Great Britain. It could be expanded to apply to other Western countries, but only to the Western ones.

In the West, economic means which operate toward world unification have become dominant. In the East, on the Communist side, political means for such unification have always been predominant. The U.S.S.R. is capable of "uniting" only that which it conquers. From this point of view not even the new regime could change anything essentially. According to its ideas, oppressed peoples are only those on whom some other government, not the Soviet one, is inflicting its rule. The Soviet

* From page 9, New York edition, Simon & Schuster, 1952.
† From page 6, *ibid.*

government subordinates its aid to others, even in the case of loans, to its political requirements.

The Soviet economy has not yet reached the point which would drive it to world unification of production. Its contradictions and difficulties stem mainly from internal sources. The system itself can still survive despite its isolation from the outside world. This is enormously expensive, but it is achieved by the widespread use of force. But this situation cannot last long; the limit must be reached. And this will be the beginning of the end of unlimited domination by the political bureaucracy, or by the new class.

Contemporary Communism could help achieve the goal of world unification most of all by political means—by internal democratization and by becoming more accessible to the outside world. However, it is still remote from this. Is it actually capable of such a thing?

What kind of picture does Communism have of itself and of the outside world?

Once, during the period of monopolies, the Marxism which Lenin modified conceived the internal and external relationships into which Czarist Russia and similar countries had fallen with a degree of accuracy. With this picture to spur it on, the movement headed by Lenin fought and won. In Stalin's time this same ideology, again modified, was realistic to the extent that it defined, almost accurately, the position and role of the new state in international relations. The Soviet state, or the new class, was in a good position externally and internally, subordinating to itself all that it could acquire.

Now the Soviet leaders have a hard time orienting themselves. They are no longer capable of seeing contemporary reality. The world which they see is not the one that really exists. It is either the one that used to exist or the one that they would wish to have exist.

Holding on to obsolete dogmas, the Communist leaders thought that all the rest of the world would stagnate and destroy itself in conflicts and struggles. This did not happen. The West advanced both economically and intellectually. It proved to be united whenever danger from another system threatened. The colonies were freed, but did not become Communist, nor did this lead to a rupture with the mother countries involved.

The breakdown of Western capitalism through crises and wars did not take place. In 1949 Vishinsky, at the United Nations, in the name of the Soviet leadership, predicted the beginning of a great new crisis in the United States and in capitalism. The opposite happened. This was not because capitalism is good or bad, but because the capitalism the Soviet leaders rant about no longer exists. The Soviet leaders could not see that India, the Arab states, and similar countries had become independent, until they began to approve—for their own reasons—Soviet points of view in foreign policy. The Soviet leaders did not and do not now understand social democracy. Instead, they measure it by the yardstick with which they measure the fate of the Social Democrats in their own area. Basing their thinking on the fact that their country did not reach the development which the Social Democrats foresaw, Soviet leaders conclude that social democracy in the West, as well, is unreal and "treacherous."

This is also true with regard to their evaluation of the basic conflict—the conflict between systems, or the basic tendency toward the unification of production. Here too their evaluation is out of focus.

They declare that this conflict is a struggle between two different social systems. In one of them—theirs, of course—they state that there are no classes, or that the classes are in the process of liquidation, and that theirs is state ownership. In the other system—the foreign one—they insist that there are raging class struggles and crises while all material goods are in the hands of private individuals, and that the government is only the tool of a handful of greedy monopolists. With this view of the world, they believe that the present conflicts would have been avoided if such relationships had not been predominant in the West.

That is where the difficulty lies.

Even if relationships in the West were the way the Communists would like them to be—the conflict would still continue. Perhaps the conflict would be even more severe in this case. For not only forms of ownership would differ; it would be a matter of different, opposing aspirations, behind which stand modern technology and the vital interests of whole nations, in which various groups, parties, and classes endeavor to have the same problem solved according to their needs.

When the Soviet leaders rate the modern Western countries as blind instruments of the monopolies, they are just as wrong as they are in interpreting their own system as a classless society where ownership is in the hands of society. Certainly the monopolies play an important role in the politics of the Western countries, but in no case is the role as great or the same as before the First World War, nor even as before the Second World War. There is, in the background, something new and more essential; an irresistible aspiration toward the unification of the world. This is now expressed more strongly through statism and nationalization—or through the role of the government in the economy—than it is through the influence and action of the monopolies.

To the extent that one class, party, or leader stifles criticism completely, or holds absolute power, it or he inevitably falls into an unrealistic, egotistical, and pretentious judgment of reality.

This is happening today to the Communist leaders. They do not control their deeds, but are forced into them by reality. There are advantages in this; they are now more practical men than they used to be. However, there are also disadvantages, because these leaders basically lack realistic, or even approximately realistic, views. They spend more time defending themselves from world reality and attacking it than they do in getting accustomed to it. Their adherence to obsolete dogma incites them to senseless actions, from which, on more mature thoughts, they constantly retreat, but with bloody heads. Let us hope that the latter will prevail with them. Certainly, if the Communists interpreted the world realistically, they might lose, but they would gain as human beings, as part of the human race.

In any case, the world will change and will go in the direction in which it has been moving and must go on—toward greater unity, progress, and freedom. The power of reality and the power of life have always been stronger than any kind of brutal force and more real than any theory.